POLYGLOTT TRAVELLER'S GUIDE

Munich

With 17 illustrations
21 maps and plans

GENERAL INTRODUCTION

Munich	3
Historical Survey	7
Art and Culture	9
Museums and Collections	12
Practical Hints	13
Accommodation in Munich	15
Food and Drink	16
Shopping	18
Evening Entertainment	19
Transport	21

WALKS THROUGH MUNICH

1. The Central City: Karlsplatz – Marienplatz ... 23
2. The Burgher's Munich: St. Peter – Sendlinger Tor – Stadtmuseum – Viktualienmarkt – Heiliggeistkirche ... 27
3. The Old City: Marienplatz – Burgstraße – Alter Hof – Münze – Post – Hofbräuhaus – Isartor – Deutsches Museum ... 30
4. Royal Munich: Max-Joseph-Platz – Nationaltheater – Residenz – Hofgarten – Former Armeemuseum ... 34
5. The City at the time of Ludwig I: Odeonsplatz – Ludwig-straße – Siegestor – Englischer Garten ... 39
6. The Buildings of the Nobility: Odeonsplatz – Wittelsbacher-platz – Promenadeplatz – Lenbachplatz – Alter Botanischer Garten ... 43
7. Munich and its Museums: Alter Botanischer Garten – St. Bonifaz – Königsplatz – Karolinenplatz – Lenbachhaus – Alte und Neue Pinakothek ... 45
8. The Extension of the City in the 19th Century: Maximilian-straße and Prinzregentenstraße ... 49
9. The West: Theresienwiese – Messegelände – Westpark ... 54

Schloß and Schloßpark Nymphenburg	55
Sights on the City Outskirts	57
Excursions in the Surrounding Areas	61
Index	64

POLYGLOTT-VERLAG

MÜNCHEN

W9-APF-725

Published by the Polyglott-Redaktion
Author: Dr. Klaus Andreas Dietsch
Translated by Dr. David C. Green
Illustrations: Vera Solymosi-Thurzó
Maps and plans: Franz Huber and Gert Oberländer
Cover photo: Andreas Tielebier-Langenscheidt

*

We thank the Fremdenverkehrsamt der
Landeshauptstadt München for their ready assistance.

Suggestions for improvements are welcome
and should be addressed to:
Polyglott-Verlag, Redaktion, Postfach 40 11 20, 8000 München 40.

All information dates from February 1983.
Every care has been taken to ensure accuracy,
but the publishers can accept no responsibility
for errors or omissions.

*

Figures and letters in square brackets
behind the names of sights refer to
the appropriate maps and plans.
Coloured figures in the margins
refer to the numbers of the walks.

*

Rating of Sights:

***Sights of first-rate importance. Just to see them alone is worth a trip.

**Important scenery, places of interest, buildings, or works of art. It is worth a detour to see them.

*Interesting sights that can be taken notice of in a country, a place or a building.

*

7th newly revised Edition 1983/84
© 1967, 1983 by Polyglott-Verlag Dr. Bolte KG, München
Printed in Germany/Druckhaus Langenscheidt, Berlin / C.IV.Zc.
ISBN 3-493-61399-7

View over Odeonsplatz, Theatinerkirche and Frauenkirche

Munich

The art of living and letting live is one of the many secrets of Munich, which for centuries has attracted people from all parts of Germany, even all Europe, and provided them a warm welcome. This secret is well expressed by Munich's official nickname: "World city with heart."

But what is Munich? Hofbräuhaus, Oktoberfest, Schwabing, Bavarian hospitality? All this is part of it. But Munich is really so much more. The city radiates an atmosphere which not only attracts strangers but also holds them. Munich has understood how to awaken those sleeping powers in the so-called "Zuagroasten" (immigrants) which allow the stranger to say: "Here I am a man, here I am allowed to be one."

Native born citizens of Munich have become a rarity. And so much greater is the number of spiritual Munich citizens. After the Second World War the Bavarian capital had the highest growth rate of all the big cities in the German Federal Republic; with regard to tourists spending the night in the city, Munich competes with other European centres like Rome, Paris, Vienna, or London. The reason is surely the atmosphere of the city also, which seems to allow the inhabitants a life style at once free, humane, and animated, as well as meaningful and unconcerned – more so than any other German city.

Munich's strength of attraction lies in the fact that its opposites can unite and its extremes can become reconciled. The most divergent philosophies of life exist peacefully side by side. Baroque zest for living is paired with deep piety. The exuberance of Fasching harmonizes with the humility of a Corpus Christi procession. Concerts by world famous conductors are of the same importance as brassband music in beer halls. Artistic works from the two Pinakotheks or the Lenbachhaus, known the world over, compete with art from the streets provided by the young artists of Schwabing.

The colourful palette of Munich life is based on 800 years of history. A sense of tradition and cosmopolitanism, the consciousness of yesterday and of life on the morrow – with such notions is the character of Munich demarcated.

Not the least of the reasons for the Bavarian capital's popularity, however, is its wonderful surroundings.

Position and Size

Munich is the capital of Bavaria and of the administrative district of Upper Bavaria. It lies on a plain belonging to the Bavarian Alpine Foreland. Munich is about 530 m (1,700 ft.) above sea level; from this point the country falls gradually towards the north until the Danube is reached. The Isar, which originates in the Alps about 90 km (55 miles) away, flows through the town from south to north. The core of the old city is on the left, western bank of the river.

At the moment approximately 1,300,000 people are living in the city, which covers about 310 sq. km (120 sq. miles). Among the inhabitants are more than 215,000 foreigners. Munich is the third largest city in Germany, trailing only Berlin and Hamburg.

Geological and Hydrographic Features

The Limestone Alps and the Alpine Foreland came into being in the tertiary period, i.e. about 70 million years ago. When the *northern Limestone Alps* – pillared in the southwest by the Zugspitze (2963 m) and in the southeast by the Watzmann (2713 m) – stratified, their northern brim lay adjacent to a sea, from the deposits of which the sandy, clayey zone of the *Alpine Foreland* originated.

During the Ice Age, however, the greater part of the Alpine Foreland was covered by masses of rubble. The northern part of the Bavarian plateau includes the highly fertile flint (or clay) area, which is no longer affected by the folding processes found in the Alps. The south is covered by morainic hills. In between there are "Schotterfelder" (fluvio-glacial outwash), like around Munich, which form a relatively unfertile area. Wherever these deposits begin to get thinner, like to the north of Munich, the ground water can permeate the gravel surface and flood the area. Marshes originate, which are called "Moose" in Bavaria. The most extensive marsh areas are around *Erdinger* and *Dachauer Moos.* After the glaciers of the Ice Age had melted, various lakes remained, the most famous of which are the *Starnberger See,* the *Ammersee,* the *Tegernsee,* and, largest of all, the *Chiemsee.*

The *Isar,* which cuts through Munich, as well as all rivers in Bavaria, flows in a northerly direction, since the country flattens out towards the Danube. The Isar originates in Tyrol as a mountain stream and cuts across the border near Mittenwald. South of Munich (near Wolfratshausen) it collects water from the *Loisach*; northeast of Munich the *Amper* flows into the Isar, before the latter finally ends by joining the Danube near Deggendorf.

Climate

Because of Munich's closeness to the northern edge of the Alps, precipitation is rather high. Rain storms often come violently and unexpectedly. The range of temperature between day and night or between summer and winter can be extreme. Even during a single season there are often drastic changes in temperature. A period of bad weather in summer can push the mercury below the level of a spring day warmed by the Föhn.

Climate Chart

Average rate for Munich

	Temp. (°C)		Sun	Precip.
	Min.	Max.	Hours	mm
Jan.	− 5,6	1,4	56	56
Febr.	− 5,1	3,4	82	51
Mar.	− 1,5	8,7	120	48
Apr.	2,8	13,5	161	61
May	6,6	18,0	187	106
June	10,0	21,3	225	124
July	12,1	23,2	240	141
Aug.	11,4	22,7	206	99
Sept.	8,4	19,6	180	86
Oct.	3,7	13,3	138	64
Nov.	0,1	6,6	57	54
Dec.	− 3,8	2,3	38	45

A famous and feared climatic feature is the *Föhn,* which manages to change not only the weather and the temperature completely within a few hours, but also the mood of the people. This warm fall wind is blamed by some people in Munich whenever they don't feel well or have a particular tendency to be grouchy. But there are enough specimens of Munich citizens believing themselves to be in top shape on a Föhn-day. The Föhn is a warm southerly wind which originates when there is a ridge of high pressure on the south side of the Alps (Italy) and a low pressure area on the north side. The warmed air rises on the south side of the Alps, dries and forms a bank of clouds along the ridges of the mountains. Because of the low-pressure area in the north of the Alps, the air is sucked from the mountains. Thus it descends as a warm wind through the Alpine Foreland as far as the Danube. In times of Föhn the Alps viewed from Munich seem within touching distance and are most clearly detailed.

Population

The so-called *"Altmünchner"* (native of Munich), who is becoming rarer and rarer, is often depicted in clichées – mostly incorrect and exaggerated – as a mixture of coarseness, craftiness, and bad temper. In reality the typical "Altmünchner" is usually a person with a baroque love of life and subtle humor. The big city Bavarian mentality is stamped by a strongly conservative ideology, the main reason for which is a deep-rooted individualism; the old Bavarian type intensely dislikes having his individuality attacked by modernistic trends.

Since the Second World War the "Altmünchner's" living space – both physically and spiritually – has been reduced by the influx of vast numbers of "Preissn" (Prussians; the name applies to all North Germans from the far side of the Main river) and refugees.

Dialect

The fact that the German population of Munich is divided almost exactly in half between "Zuagroasten" (immigrants) and native inhabitants can be clearly heard in speech. Everywhere in the city what is called *Munich High German* can be heard – speech corresponding to the other forms of written German in vocabulary and syntax, but differing in accent.

The *old-Bavarian dialect* is linguistically more similar to the language spoken in Austria (both have as ancestors the Germanic Baiuwarii) than to the Swabian dialect, which is derived from Alemannic.

Religion

Munich is a predominantly Roman Catholic city and has been the seat of the *Archbishop of Munich and Freising* since 1821. Religious observances play an important role for many of the people and most of the customs which still colour the seasons of the year have their roots in Catholic piety. The Protestant population has grown immensely through the influx of refugees and North Germans. There are now about 320,000 Protestants in Munich, as well as a relatively large Jewish community.

Festivities

Tradition and custom are at the root of the Munich festivities. The Munich calendar opens with

Fasching (January 7th until Ash Wednesday). This expression is of Austrian-Bavarian origin and means "night of fasting". This time of unconcerned exuberance has the same origin as the Rhenish carnival, but is probably based on pre-Christian festivals greeting the return of spring. Masquerades, glitter, and flirting are trump. The artists' balls in Schwabing are particularly outstanding, as well as the activities of Fasching organizations, press and film balls, and the dances of the "Damische Ritter" – the "daft knights" – or the "Vorstadthochzeit" – the "suburban wedding". On Fasching Sunday, the Sunday before Ash Wednesday, the word is "Foolish Munich". In the afternoon a great public Fasching festival takes place between Marienplatz and Karlstor. On Fasching Tuesday (Shrove Tuesday) in the morning the market women dance at the Viktualienmarkt, while in the afternoon there is unrestrained activity all through the central city.

Starkbierzeit (the strong beer season) begins in March (around St. Joseph's Day). The Munich breweries serve a special kind of brown beer in a strictly observed ceremony. This beer has a maximal alcohol content of 6%. The most popular centres of attraction are the Salvatorkeller, on the Nockherberg, and the Löwenbräukeller, where Bavaria's strong men test their strength against Steirer Hans's 560 lb. stone.

Auer Dult. This market and fair, which takes place three times a year, in spring, summer and autumn, is held at Mariahilf-platz in the Au quarter. In addition to the usual pleasures like roundabouts, there is a second-hand market.

Maibock (or May beer). This pure and somewhat bright brown beer without additional coloured malt closes out the Starkbierzeit (strong beer season). Originally Maibock came from northern Germany, to be exact from Einbeck in Lower Saxony. Duke Wilhelm V, who founded the Hofbräuhaus in 1589, had his master brewer brought from there. In 1614 Elias Pichler presented this "ain pöckisch" (= Einbeckisch) drink for the first time, whose sale was a special privilege of the court until 1818. The testing of the Maibock (usually around the end of

April) is regarded as an "official act of state".

Fronleichnam (Corpus Christi – second Thursday after Whitsun). The Roman Catholic Corpus Christi procession is a particularly magnificent demonstration in Munich. It begins traditionally at 8 a.m. with a communal religious service at Marienplatz.

The Summer Festival (July and August). At the centre of the so-called "Festive Summer" is the Opera festival with conductors and singers of international reputation at the National Theatre. Concerts in the Nymphenburg Palace, the Ballet Week Festival, Lieder recitals, evenings in the Herkulessaal and matinées in the Cuvilliés Theatre respectively, as well as concerts in the Brunnenhof of the Residence round out this highlight of musical life.

Oktoberfest (middle of September until first Sunday in October). A horse race at the wedding of Crown Prince Ludwig (later King Ludwig I) to Princess Therese von Sachsen-Hildburghausen in 1810 signalled the birth of the present giant fair. Until well into the middle of the 19th century horse races and shooting contests remained highlights of the festival. But since that time the more popular attractions such as roller coaster, Ferris wheels, and house of horrors, etc., have become increasingly prevalent. Today the "Wies'n", as the Munich citizens call their popular festival at the Theresienwiese, attracts some 5 million people per year, who drink more than 4 million litres of beer during the sixteen days of the festival. The Oktoberfest begins when the mayor drives in the first beer tap. The main attractions are the procession of Wies'n brewers and innkeepers with their splendidly decorated beer wagons and the great Bavarian costume parade on the first festival Sunday.

Christkindlmarkt (the three weeks before Christmas). At Marienplatz and the connecting streets of the pedestrian zone wares related to Christmas are sold.

Government and Administration

Munich is the capital of Bavaria and of the administrative district of Upper Bavaria. For this reason it is the seat of many institutions: the Landtag (Parliament), the Senate, the Bavarian State Government, the Highest Bavarian Law Court, the Bavarian Constitutional Court, the Bavarian Administrative Court, the District Council, the Government of Upper Bavaria. Also included are several federal offices such as the Federal Finance Audit Office, the German Patent Office (Munich is even the seat of the European Patent Office). Furthermore, the city is also the seat of various religious dignitaries.

Economy

Munich is the third largest *industrial city* in the German Federal Republic. Names like Siemens, BMW, Krauss-Maffei, MAN, Rathgeber, MBB, Zündapp, Linhof, and Rodenstock are closely connected with Munich. Of considerable economic importance are also the Munich breweries. There are 6 major breweries. The above-mentioned companies are supplemented by important chemical, printing, and clothing industries.

The significance of Munich as a financial centre is proven by its more than 100 *banks*. There are also 35 *insurance companies* situated here. Because of numerous special exhibitions, Munich is regarded as the *international centre* in this field, too.

Handicrafts are still an important economic factor. Approximately 130,000 employees work in some 12,000 businesses.

With 300 firms *producing books* Munich has the most publishing houses of any city in the Federal Republic of Germany.

Knowledge and Research

The *Ludwig-Maximilian University* has about 42,000 students and the *Technical University* more than 16,000. In addition to these two universities there are the Military Academy, the School of Philosophy, the State Academy of Music, the Academy for Television and Film, the Academy for Pictorial Art, the Bavarian Academy of Science and the Bavarian Academy of the Fine Arts, as well as numerous technical schools. Of great significance are the Max Planck Institutes for Physics and Astrophysics, Biochemestry, and Cell Chemistry, and others; among them excels the Institute for Atomic Research in Garching.

The largest library in the German Federal Republic is the *Bavarian State Library*, with more than 4 million books, followed by the University Library (2 million books).

Historical Survey

Münchner Kindl

About 1200 B.C. the *Illyrians,* who had come from southeast Europe, settled on the north edge of the Alps. From the 5th century B.C. *Celts* penetrated the Alpine Foreland from the west.

15 B.C. The *Romans* under Tiberius and Drusus thrust forward to the Danube.

C. 500 A.D. After a short *Ostrogothic rule,* the country begins to be settled by the *Baiuwarii* from Bohemia.

746 The *monastery at Tegernsee* is founded, a small branch of which on the Isar is given the name "Munichen" (the home of the monks). The name first appears in a document in 777.

912 *Arnulf* (whose house is named after his residence, the Castle Wittelsbach) succeeds in renewing the local dukedom.

947 Bavaria falls to the Saxons under Emperor *Otto I,* who delegates the duchy to his brother *Heinrich.*

1070 The *Welfs* become dukes of Bavaria.

1158 *Henry the Lion,* the last and most famous of the Welf dukes, founds Munich. In 1156 he destroys the bridge over the Isar at Oberföhring (which belongs to the bishop of Freising and brings in a vast toll) and builds a new one a few miles up river near Munichen, where he collects the toll himself. The brisk salt transport from Reichenhall and Hallein assure a profitable income.

Henry the Lion moves with coinage and market to Munichen. After Emperor *Frederick I Barbarossa* sanctions the results of Henry's manœuvring at the Reichstag (imperial diet) in Augsburg, Munich is born. The official date: June 14th, 1158.

1180 Henry the Lion falls under the imperial ban for denying Frederick Barbarossa military obedience. The Hohenstaufen emperor rewards his loyal vassal *Otto von Wittelsbach* with the duchy of Bavaria.

1255 Duke *Ludwig II* (the Stern) receives the Palatinate and Upper Bavaria as his part in the first partition of Bavaria. He makes Munich his residence.

1302 Duke *Ludwig the Bavarian* begins his rule (from 1314 German king, from 1328 emperor). He builds a second ring of walls around Munich; the construction takes 15 years.

1327 Munich falls victim to a devastating fire.

1392 The third partition of Bavaria occurs. The country is divided into the dukedoms of Ingolstadt, Landshut, and Munich.

1397 A rising of the guilds, which is repeated several times in the succeeding period, helps the burghers to take over the government of the town to an increasing extent.

1429 Part of the town is burnt down.

1506 Duke *Albrecht IV* (the Wise) issues a decree enforcing primogeniture, thereby initiating the end of Bavaria's partition. Munich become the capital of the whole of Bavaria.

1508—1550 Duke *Wilhelm IV* reigns. During his rule the Reformation is introduced in Bavaria, against which particularly the Jesuits were bitterly opposed.

1550—1579 Duke *Albrecht V* puts an end to the religious strife by initiating the "exclusive Catholicy of Bavaria". The duke encourages art and learning. He brings famous foreign artists to the court (among them *Orlando di Lasso*) and founds the Munich Court Library which was to form the nucleus of the Bavarian State Library.

1597 Duke *Maximilian I* becomes ruler of Bavaria. In 1609 he founds the

7

Catholic League, which he leads during the Thirty Years' War. From 1623 until his death Maximilian rules under the title Elector of Bavaria.

1632 King *Gustavus Adolphus of Sweden* occupies Munich with his soldiers.

1634 The imperial Spanish troops enter Munich. Plague and the confusions of the Thirty Years' War decimate the population, which sinks from 22,000 to 9,000.

1704—1714 In the War of the Spanish Succession Elector *Maximilian II Emanuel,* who takes sides with France, loses the whole of Bavaria to the Austrians. Peasants under the leadership of the *Smith from Kochel* rise against the Austrian occupying force, only to be massacred by imperial troops in "the murderous Christmas of Sendling". Maximilian II Emanuel receives Bavaria back without loss of territory at the peace conference of 1714.

1742 The Wittelsbach Karl Albrecht is elected Emperor in Frankfurt as *Karl VII.*

1745—1777 His son *Maximilian III* rules in Bavaria. He makes peace with Austria, renouncing his hereditary titles and assures three decades of peace, devoting himself to the demands of learning and the construction of his state.

1779—1799 *Karl Theodor* from the line of Rudolph (the Palatinate) rules from Munich a Bavaria that includes the Upper Palatinate but not the Innviertel.

1799—1825 Bavaria is ruled by *Maximilian IV Joseph* from the Palatinate-Zweibrücken line. As compensation for areas left of the Rhine (incorporated with Bavaria by Karl Theodor) ceded to Napoleon, Bavaria receives the secularized bishoprics Würzburg, Bamberg, Augsburg, Freising, and Passau at a peace conference with France in 1803.

1805 *Napoleon* makes Munich his headquarters. After the battle of Austerlitz he transfers to Bavaria the margravate Ansbach – Bayreuth, as well as the Austrian territories of Vorarlberg, Tyrol, Salzburg, Innviertel and Hausruckviertel.

1806 Maximilian VI Joseph receives the title king as a favour from Napoleon and calls himself from now on *Maximilian I Joseph.*

1815 Bavaria joins the *German Confederation.*

1818 Maximilian I Joseph proclaims the Bavarian constitution.

1825 King *Ludwig I* comes to the throne. Under his rule Munich becomes a brilliant centre of art and learning.

1840 The railway line from Munich to Augsburg is opened.

1848 The revolution of 1848, particularly caused in Bavaria by the king's love affair with a young dancer named *Lola Montez,* leads to Ludwig I's abdication.

1848—1864 His son *Maximilian II* reigns. He fosters art and learning and introduces important innovations in the sphere of social reform.

1864—1886 marks the reign of King *Ludwig II,* the storybook king, builder of fantastic castles. Under him Bavaria takes the side of Austria in the Seven Weeks' War against Prussia (1866) and that of Prussia in the Franco-German War (1870—1871).

1886—1912 Prince Regent *Luitpold* rules in place of Ludwig's mentally disturbed brother.

1918 The last reigning Wittelsbach, King *Ludwig III,* is deposed by the revolutionary *Kurt Eisner* in the November revolution. Since that time Bavaria has been a republic and is called "Free State".

1923 An attempted National Socialist (Nazi) Putsch is severely put down in front of the Feldherrnhalle.

1933 The *National Socialists* remove the last legally elected city council on March 9th. Munich becomes the "capital of the Nazi movement".

1938 The *Munich Agreement,* signed here by Hitler, Mussolini, Chamberlain, and Daladier, seals the destruction of Czechoslovakia.

1943 A gallant group of university students and professors, known as the *White Rose,* revolt against the tyranny of the Third Reich.

1945 Munich is taken by American troops without resistance.

1946 The constitution of the Bavarian Free State is approved by the people.

1957 The population of Munich exceeds the one million mark.

1972 The *XXth Olympic Games* are held.

1972—1980 Extension of underground lines.

1983 *International Horticulture Exhibition* at the Westpark grounds.

Art and Culture

Architecture

There are only a few *Romanesque* buildings surviving in Bavaria and in Munich none at all.

The *Gothic* period is represented by the Frauenkirche, the Altes Rathaus (the Old Town Hall) and the Alter Hof (the Old Court), the first seat of the Bavarian dukes in Munich. Between 1468 and his death (1488) the town architect Jörg Ganghofer built the Frauenkirche with its "welschen Hauben" ("Guelph bonnets"), the twin cupolas of the cathedral crowning the towers (one 100 m high, the other 99). The church is one of the last late-Gothic churches with a great hallway in Germany. Between 1470 and 1474 Ganghofer incorporated parts of an earlier town hall into the Gothic construction of the Altes Rathaus at Marienplatz. The Alter Hof dates from the time of Ludwig the Stern (1253–1294). Particularly worthy of notice are also the stylistically pure churches in the west part of the city: the Palace Chapel Blutenburg (1488) and the Parish Church St. Wolfgang at Pipping (1478–1480).

The *Renaissance* is represented by three large edifices in Munich: the Münzhof (inner court of the mint; 1563–1567), surrounded by three-storey arcades, was built by Wilhelm Egkl; Friedrich Sustris was responsible for Michaelskirche (1583–1597) and the Maximilian Residence. Between 1569 and 1571 Sustris, together with the Italian Jacobo Strada and Wilhelm Egkl, had erected the Antiquarium. From 1613 to 1616 Sustris worked together with Peter Candid and Hans Krumper.

Baroque architecture was introduced in Munich under Elector Ferdinand Maria, who laid the foundation for the Theatinerkirche (St. Kajetan); construction was started by the Italian Agostino Barelli and continued by his compatriot Enrico Zuccalli. The Theatinerkirche, with its tambour and cupola, gave Munich its first touch of Italian splendour. The Dreifaltigkeitskirche (Trinity Church) was built between 1711 and 1718 by Giovanni Antonio Viscardi. The brothers Asam constructed the Johann-Nepomuk-Kirche from 1733 to 1746. St. Michael in Berg am Laim was built by Johann Michael Fischer from 1738 to 1751. Elector Ferdinand Maria allowed Barelli to begin construction on the Nymphenburg Palace in 1664, which his son Maximilian II Emanuel had expanded under Joseph Effner. This architect also finished the New Palace in Schleißheim from 1719 to 1726, a project begun in 1701 by Zuccalli under Max Emanuel's patronage. Zuccalli was earlier responsible for Lustheim Palace in Schleißheim (1684–1688). The architect François Cuvilliés is also connected with Nymphenburg – there he created the Hall of Mirrors and the Amalienburg in true rococo spirit. A jewel of rococo is the Old Residence Theatre or Cuvilliés Theatre.

In the *19th century* Munich changed from merely a simple city of residence to a true city of art. Ludwig I gave the order for his collection of classical art in the Glyptothek Museum and for the Wittelsbach Collection in the Old and New Pinakothek. The National Theatre, originally constructed by Karl von Fischer 1811 and 1818, was rebuilt after a fire by Leo von Klenze, Ludwig's court architect, between 1823 and 1825. Klenze, along with Friedrich von Gärtner, the sculptor Ludwig Schwanthaler and the painter Peter Cornelius, gave shape to the "Maxvorstadt" (Max suburb), the expansion between Munich and Schwabing, with Ludwigstraße ("via triumphalis") as main artery. The Residence received its final form, the Feldherrnhalle and Siegestor were erected. Under Maximilian II, who in his plan to expand the city insisted on consistancy with a "new style", Maximilianstraße was laid down. The crowning touch at the end of the street is the Maximilianeum, on the other side of the Isar. The last major expansion of Munich planned as an ensemble was Prinzregentenstraße. The patron, Prince Regent Luitpold, used some of Ludwig II's former architectural plans, which had been set aside for lack of funds. The Bavarian National Museum was constructed between 1894 and 1900 by Gabriel von Seidl, Adolf von Hildebrand and Jakob Möhl did work on the Friedensengel (Angel of Peace).

After the Second World War Munich was cleared of rubble and converted into a city suitable to motor-car traffic by widening the streets. Only the old city can be considered truly atmospheric and friendly. The Olympic Park and many modern buildings give the city a new accent.

Sculpture

Gothic influence in sculpture begins to be felt only from about 1400. During the construction of the Frauenkirche, local artists began to appear, although at this time and for the following centuries foreign artists or artists who had made their reputations in the Bavarian surroundings were again and again brought to Munich. This was also true for that superb master

Moresque dancer

of late-Gothic from the Upper Palatinate, Erasmus Grasser (1450–1518), who was commissioned to decorate the Altes Rathaus (Old Town Hall).

Although in the *Renaissance* works of art were produced by native masters like Hans Asslinger or Caspar Weinhart, the most significant pieces of sculpture were made by Italian and Dutch artists. Among the latter was Hubert Gerhard, who designed the statue of Mary on the Mariensäule (Virgin's Column), as well as the Perseus Fountain in the Residence. Hans Krumper was the guiding light in the field of sculpture at the turn of the 17th century. He produced among other things the "Patrona Boiariae" on the west side of the Residence.

In the *baroque period* Bavarian sculptors were the most prominent, but they had all studied in Italy. A short list of a much longer one: Tobias Pader, Balthasar Ableithner, Andreas Feistenberger, Ägid Quirin Asam, Johann Baptist Straub, Ignaz Günther, and Roman Anton Boos, who made a name for himself primarily in sacred art.

19th century Munich sculpture bears the stamp of Ludwig Schwanthaler, a pupil of Bertel Thorvaldsen and Christian Rauch, sculptors brought to Munich by Ludwig I. Schwanthaler created the giant statue of Bavaria at the Theresienwiese, a masterpiece in bronze, cast by Ferdinand von Miller. High perfection in bronze technique is also demonstrated by the Quadriga on top of the Siegestor, a creation of Johann Halbig and Johann Martin von Wagner. At the end of the 19th century Adolf von Hildebrand was the leading sculptor. Kaspar von Zumbusch and Franz von Stuck were also important.

Painting

The few works from *Romanesque times* come from anonymous masters. Such is the case in the initial painting from the manuscripts of Emperor Ludwig of Bavaria, done in the Italian style, and the table panel pair (ca. 1400) representing the "Crucifixion of Christ" and the "Resurrection of Drusiana" (in the Bavarian National Museum).

Painting in Munich reached its first high point in the *late-Gothic period*. In the second half of the 15th century Jan Polack from Crakow painted the frescoes of St. Wolfgang in Pipping, worked on the high altar of the Peterskirche and on the altars of the Palace Chapel Blutenburg. Polack made many designs for glass windows in the Frauenkirche. Peter Hemmel von Andlau is also famous for his stained glass painting on the windows of the church.

After Munich had stood for some years in the shadow of Nuremberg (Albrecht Dürer) and Regensburg (Albrecht Altdorfer), there developed *as of 1530* under Wilhelm IV a court art, the paintings of which provided the fundament for the Wittelsbach Collection. Ludwig Reflinger, Hans Burgkmair, Jörg Breu, Melchior Feselen, and Barthel Beham worked on this cycle of historical pictures. Hans Mielich (1516–1573) was an important personage, who especially excelled in portrait painting. Wilhelm V brought Friedrich Sustris to his court, along with a man from Brügge named de Wit, more widely known as Peter Candid.

Johann Heinrich Schönfeld, Joachim von Sandrart, Johann Carl Loth and Johann Andreas Wolff are worthy exponents for art of the *17th century*. The names Cosmas Damian Asam and Georges de Marées are connected with the rococo period.

In the *19th century* a Munich painting tradition developed, in which Wilhelm von Kobell, Peter von Cornelius, Wilhelm von Kaulbach and Karl von Piloty are regarded as the most famous representatives. Johann Georg von Dillis and Carl Rottmann made names for themselves as landscape painters. Carl Spitzweg concentrated on the "Idyll". The leading influences at the end of the 19th century came from Franz von Lenbach, Friedrich August von Kaulbach, Franz von Stuck, as well as Wilhelm Leibl.

Characteristic of the early *20th century* were the Munich artist groups. In 1909 Wassily Kandinsky initiated the "New Artist Group of Munich", which Alexej von Jawlensky, Paul Klee, Alfred Kubin, August Macke, Franz Marc, and Gabriele Münter all joined. Due to differences of opinion the group broke up in 1911 and a new group called "Der Blaue Reiter" gathered around Kandinsky.

Literature

In the *13th and 14th century* several historiographers were at work in Munich. The Emperor Ludwig the Bavarian (1314–1347) founded a scholarly academy to which philosophers such as William of Occam and Marsilius of Padua belonged. Bavarian humanism was represented by Nikolaus Kratzer (born in Munich in 1487).

The Munich theatre was already developing into a powerful medium of expression at the end of the *16th century*. The Counter-Reformation brought a specifically Bavarian literary form in the Jesuit drama. In 1602 Jakob Bidermann wrote one of its chief works, "Cenodoxus, Doctor from Paris". From 1722 onwards a group of Augustinian monks published the "Parnassus Boicus", a literary organ which was concerned with the preservation and purification of the German language. This was the basis of the Bavarian Academy.

In the *19th century* under Maximilian II Munich reached a literary high point. An important group of poets called the "Bund der Krokodile" (Crocodile Club) was formed around Paul Heyse and Emanuel Geibel. The king also brought first-class minds such as Friedrich Wilhelm von Schelling, Leopold von Ranke and Wilhelm von Giesebrecht to Munich.

From the *turn of the century up to the twenties* the city attracted literary figures like Henrik Ibsen, Stefan George, Rainer Maria Rilke, Frank Wedekind, Heinrich and Thomas Mann, as well as Ludwig Thoma and Oskar Maria Graf. Later on came Bertolt Brecht and Erich Kästner. Today's literary scene is dominated by people like Carl Amery, Franz Xaver Kroetz, Angelika Mechtel and Herbert Rosendorfer.

Music

In *1482* a church choir was founded in Munich and musical life in this period was influenced by the blind organist and composer Konrad Paumann. In *1526* the Swiss musician Ludwig Senfl became leader of the court orchestra, and from 1556 till 1594 this position was held by Orlando di Lasso, one of the great figures of Renaissance music.

In the *17th century* the Italian opera was established in Munich. In the *18th century* Wolfgang Amadeus Mozart tried without success to enter the service of the court. His operas "La finta giardiniera" and "Idomeneo" were first performed in Munich, but were treated harshly by the critics.

In the second half of the *19th century* under Ludwig II, the Munich opera along with Bayreuth became the bearer of the artistic ideas of Richard Wagner. In 1901 Max Reger left the Upper Palatinate to

BMW tower

come to Munich. Hans Pfitzner taught from 1929 onwards at the Akademie der Tonkunst (Academy of Musical Art). Richard Strauss was Munich's "great son". After the Second World War the music scene was dominated by Carl Orff, Werner Egk and Karl Amadeus Hartmann.

Museums and Collections

***Alte Pinakothek,** Barer Straße 27 (north door), Tel. 23 80 52 16. Open daily except Mon. 9 a.m. – 4.30 p.m., Tues. and Thurs. also 7–9 p.m. Admission charge, Sun, and holidays free (see p. 46).

Neue Pinakothek, Barer Straße 29 (entrance Theresienstraße), Tel. 23 80 50. Open daily except Mon. 9 a.m. – 4.30 p.m., Tues. also 7–9 p.m. Admission charge, Sun. and holidays free (see p. 47).

Staatsgalerie moderner Kunst, Haus der Kunst (west wing), Prinzregentenstraße 1, Tel. 29 27 10. Open daily except Mon. 9 a.m. – 4.30 p.m., Thurs. also 7–9 p.m. Admission charge, Sun. and holidays free (see p. 51).

*Schackgalerie,** Prinzregentenstraße 9, Tel. 22 44 07. Open daily except Tues. 9 a.m. – 4.30 p.m. Admission charge, Sun. and holidays free (see p. 53).

Staatliche Antikensammlungen, Collection of classical art, Königsplatz 1, Tel. 59 83 59. Open daily except Mon. 10 a.m. – 4.30 p.m., Wed. 12–8 p.m. Admission charge (see p. 46).

*Glyptothek,** Königsplatz 3, Tel. 28 61 00. Open daily except Mon. 10 a.m. – 4.30 p.m., Thurs. 12–8 p.m. Admission charge (see p. 45).

*Schatzkammer der Residenz,** The Royal Treasury, Max-Joseph-Platz 3, Tel. 22 46 41. Open Tues.–Sat. 10 a.m. – 4.30 p.m., Sun. and holidays 10 a.m. – 1 p.m. Admission charge (see p. 36).

*Residenzmuseum,** Max-Joseph-Platz 3, Tel. 22 46 41. Open Tues.–Sat. 10 a.m. – 4.30 p.m., Sun. and holidays 10 a.m. – 1 p.m. It includes the Altes Residenztheater (Cuvilliés-Theater), open weekdays 2–5 p.m., Sun. and holidays 10 a.m. – 5 p.m. Admission charge (see p. 36).

*Staatliche Graphische Sammlung,** State collection of the Graphic Arts, Meiserstraße 10, Tel. 55 91/3 41. Open Mon.–Fri. 9 a.m. – 1 p.m. and 2–4.30 p.m. Admission free (see p. 45).

*Staatliche Sammlung Ägyptischer Kunst,** State collection of Egyptian art, Hofgartenstraße 1, Tel. 29 85 46. Open daily except Mon. 9.30 a.m. – 4 p.m., Tues. also 7–9 p.m. Admission charge, Sun. and holidays free (see p. 38).

Staatliche Münzsammlung, State collection of coins, Residenzstraße 1, Tel. 22 72 21. Open daily except Mon. 10 a.m. – 4 p.m. Admission charge, Sun. and holidays free (see p. 36).

Staatliches Museum für Völkerkunde, State Ethnological Museum, Maximilianstraße 42, Tel. 22 48 44. Open daily except Mon. 9.30 a.m. – 4.30 p.m. Admission charge, Sun. and holidays free (see p. 49).

Burgmuseum Grünwald, Zeillerstraße 3, Tel. 6 41 32 18. Open Wed.–Sun. 10 a.m. – 4 p.m. (see p. 61).

Bayerisches Nationalmuseum, Bavarian National Museum, Prinzregentenstraße 3, Tel. 2 16 81. Open daily except Mon. 9.30 a.m. – 4.30 p.m., Sat., Sun., and holidays 10 a.m. – 4.30 p.m. Admission charge, Sun. and holidays free (see p. 52).

*Die Neue Sammlung,** The New Collection, Prinzregentenstraße 3, Tel. 22 78 44. Open daily except Mon. 10 a.m. – 5 p.m. Admission charge.

*Prähistorische Staatssammlung,** Prehistoric State Collection, Lerchenfeldstraße 2, Tel. 29 39 11. Open daily except Mon. 10 a.m. – 4 p.m., Thurs. until 8 p.m. Admission charge, Sun. and holidays free (see p. 53).

*Städtische Galerie im Lenbachhaus,** Luisenstraße 33, Tel. 52 10 41. Open daily except Mon. 9 a.m. – 4.30 p.m., Tues. until 8 p.m. Admission charge, Sun. and holidays free (see page 46).

Münchner Stadtmuseum, Municipal museum, Sankt-Jakobs-Platz 1, Tel. 2 33/23 70. Open daily except Mon. 9 a.m. – 4.30 p.m. Admission charge, Sun. and holidays free. The museum also houses a *collection of musical instruments,* the *photographic and film museum,* the *German brewery museum* and a *puppet theatre collection* (see p. 29).

***Deutsches Museum,** on the Isarinsel (Ludwigsbrücke), Tel. 2 17 91. Open daily 9 a.m. – 5 p.m. Admission charge (see p. 32).

Deutsches Jagd- und Fischereimuseum, German Hunting and Fishing Museum, Neuhauser Straße 53, Tel. 22 05 22. Open daily except Mon. 9.30 a.m. – 4 p.m. Admission charge (see p. 25).

Deutsches Theatermuseum, Galeriestraße 4a, Tel. 22 24 49. Open Tues.–Thurs. 9 a.m. – 12 and 1–4.30 p.m., Fri. until 3.30 p.m.

Mineralogische Staatssammlung, State collection of mineralogy, Theresienstraße 41 (entrance Barer Straße), Tel. 23 94-1. Open Tues.–Fri. 1–5 p.m., Sat. and Sun. 1–6 p.m. Admission charge.

BMW-Museum, Petuelring 130 (opposite the Olympia Park), Tel. 38 95 33 07. Open daily 9 a.m. – 5 p.m. Admission free (see p. 59).

Siemens-Museum, Prannerstraße 10, Tel. 2 34/26 60. Open Mon.–Fri. 9 a.m. – 4 p.m., Sat. and Sun. 10 a.m. – 2 p.m. Tours for groups can be arranged. Admission free.

Valentin-Musäum, tower of Isartor, Tel. 22 32 66. Open Mon., Tues., Sat. 11.01 a.m. – 5.29 p.m., Sun. 10.01 a.m. – 5.29 p.m. Admission charge (see p. 32). Karl Valentin was a popular Munich folkcomedian.

All state and municipal museums and collections are closed on Jan. 1st, Good Friday, Easter Sunday, the Tuesday after Easter, May 1st, Corpus Christi, Whit Sunday, the Tuesday after Whitsun, Nov. 1st, as well as Dec. 24th and 25th.

Practical Hints

Motorists

Car-piloting services (which also provide information about hotel accomodation) are available on Autobahn exits. An hour of car-piloting service with passenger guide costs 26 DM, with guide driving ahead 28 DM.

Car-piloting stations are in Freimann (Autobahn Nürnberg; Tel. 32 54 17), Obermenzing (Autobahn Stuttgart; Tel. 8 11 24 12), Ramersdorf (Autobahn Salzburg; Tel. 67 27 55) and Unterdill (Autobahn Garmisch; Tel. 75 63 30).

Banks and Exchange

Foreign currency can be changed into German Marks in all banks and saving banks, as well as in large hotels. Banks are usually open from 8.30 a.m. to 12.30 p.m. and from 1.45 to 4 p.m. (Thursday until 5.30 p.m.) There are exchange offices, which are also open on weekends, at the main train station (open 6.30 a.m. − 11.30 p.m.) and two at the airport (open 7.00 a.m. − 8.30 p.m. 7.30 a.m. − 10 p.m. resp.).

Bavaria Film Tours

Bavariafilmplatz 7, Geiselgasteig. With the film express through the Bavaria grounds. Main attractions are the ,,Berliner Straße", scene of many films, the U-boat, world-famous from the film ,,The Boat", and the mine ,,Rote Erde", typical for Ruhr district. Tours from April 1st through Oct. 31st, daily from 9 a.m. to 4 p.m. Admission fee: 8 DM for adults, 4.50 DM for children, school classes and handicapped persons.

Visiting breweries

Possible with appointment. Augustiner-Bräu (Tel. 50 30 96), Hacker-Pschorr-Bräu (Tel. 5 10 61), Hofbräuhaus (Tel. 4 48 83 44), Löwenbräu (Tel. 5 20 01), Paulaner-Salvator-Thomasbräu (Tel. 4 11 51), Spaten-Franziskaner-Bräu (Tel. 5 12 21).

Information and Accomodation

Fremdenverkehrsamt München, Municipal Tourist Office, Rindermarkt 5, advice provided in all questions of staying in Munich, Tel. 23 91-1.

Accomodation Service and Information in the main train station, Tel. 2 39 12 55-2 60, open Mon.−Sat. 8.30 a.m. − 11 p.m., Sun. 1−9.30 p.m. (no telephone accomodation service), at the airport (in the arrival hall), Tel. 90 72 56 and 2 39 12 66, open Mon.−Sat. 8.30 a.m. − 10 p.m., Sun. 11 a.m. − 7 p.m. (no flight information, no telephone accomodation service).

Branch of the Municipal Tourist Office in the subterranean shopping centre of Karlsplatz (Stachus), Tel. 2 33-82 42 or 55 44 59, open Mon.−Fri. 8 a.m. − 6 p.m.

Fremdenverkehrsverband München-Oberbayern e. V., Sonnenstraße 10, III, Tel. 59 73 47-48.

ADAC (German Automobile Association), Gau Südbayern (district Southern Bavaria), Sendlinger-Tor-Platz 9, Tel. 51 71-2 22.

Deutscher Touring Automobil Club (DTC), Amalienburgstraße 23, Tel. 8 11 10 48.

Deutscher Camping-Club e. V., Mandlstraße 28, Tel. 33 40 21.

Deutscher Alpenverein, Praterinsel 5, Tel. 29 49 40 (Alpine information).

Flight information: Tel. 92 11-21 27.

Train information: Tel. 59 29 91 and 59 33 21.

Breakdown service: ADAC, Tel. 76 76-76; ACE, Tel. 53 65 02; DTC, Tel. 8 11 12 12.

Taxi: General phone nummer 21 61-1 (see p. 22).

Markets and Flea Markets

Munich's most famous market for foodstuffs is the Viktualienmarkt in the centre of the city, very close to Marienplatz. Other permanent markets for foodstuffs are the Haidhauser Markt (Wiener Platz), the Pasinger Viktualienmarkt (Bäckerstraße) and the Schwabinger Markt (Elisabethplatz).

Flea markets. Information is provided by the Tourist Office in the subterranean shopping centre of Karlsplatz (Stachus), Tel. 2 33-82 42.

Germany's largest second-hand market is found at Kirchenstraße in Haidhausen.

Parking

There are large parking garages in the inner city at the following locations:

Underground garage Max-Joseph-Platz (in front of the Nationaltheater, capacity: 440 cars), *Parking house Färbergraben* (520 cars), *Parking house Stachus* (450 cars), *Parking garage Stachus* (entrance Herzog-Wilhelm-Straße; 800 cars), *Parking levels in the Hauptbahnhof* (250 cars), *Parking garages at the Hauptbahnhof* (Marsstraße 11; 750 cars), *Parking house at St.-Jakobs-Platz* (850 cars), *Parking garage at the Hofbräuhaus* (488 cars), *Parking garage Isartorplatz* (422 cars), *Parking garage Marienplatz* (280 cars).

Sightseeing Tours

Guided sightseeing tours are run regularly by the *Münchner Fremdenrundfahrten OHG,* main railway station (Tel. 59 04-3 14). The tours begin at Bahnhofsplatz (opposite the main entrance of the main station).

Short tour (one hour), daily 10 a.m. and 2.30 p.m. Price 10 DM.

Extended tour (c. 2½ hours) with the ascent of the Olympia Tower, daily 10 a.m. and 2.30 p.m. Price 18 DM.

Long Tour (2½ hours), daily (except Mon.) 10 a.m., including a visit to the Frauenkirche (cathedral) and the Alte Pinakothek; daily (except Mon.) 2.30 p.m., including a visit to the Nymphenburg Palace and the Residence Treasury (Sun. only the Palace and Amalienburg). Price 20 DM.

Munich by night (c. 5 hours), from Jan. 1st until Nov. 30th daily, otherwise Fri. and Sat., at 7.30 p.m. Tour includes visits to three typical night clubs. Price including dinner 90 DM.

Municipal Transport

Münchner Verkehrs- und Tarifverbund (MVV), Thierschstraße 2, Tel. 2 38 03-1. The transport area of the MVV is divided into six ring-shaped zones, the first two include the inner city and the others the outskirts. Tickets are uniform and are valid for all U- and S-trains, buses and trams. The prices depend on the number of zones resp. "Zahlgrenzen" (fare stages) crossed, which are shown on a plan displayed at every stop. For a visit of the town a *24-hour ticket* is recommended (see p. 22). The ticket need only be stamped once at the start.

Sports

Mountaineering: A great number of organized tours and mountaineering trips are offered not only by mountaineering organizations (Alpenverein and Naturfreunde) but also by large sport shops (Scheck, Schuster).

Golf: There are extensive golf links in Thalkirchen-Hinterbrühl, in Straßlach and in Feldafing at the Starnberger See.

Horse Racing: Trotting races take place in Daglfing Wed. and Sun. (sometimes Sat.). Galloping races are held weekly at Riem.

Riding: The Bavarian Riding Academy is situated in Riem. Daily rides (except Mon.) take place at the University Riding School (Königinstraße), at the Würmtal riding club (Gräfelfing), in the Sport-Scheck-Allwetteranlage (Oberföhring), and in Dirnismaning.

Swimming: There is a number of indoor and outdoor swimming pools, as well as possibilities to swim in the Isar. Information is provided by the Municipal Tourist Office (see page 13).

Tennis: In all parts of the city there are several tennis courts and clubs. For information apply to the Städtisches Sportamt (Tel. 2 33-62 24).

Important Telephone Numbers

Police	110
Fire-brigade	112
Rescue service	22 26 66
Pharmacy emergency service	59 44 75
Medical emergency service	55 86 61
ADAC-information	28 01 01
Lost and found office	2 33-35 08

Services for English-Speaking Visitors

Consulates: American Consulate, Königinstraße 5, Munich 22, Tel. 2 30 11.

British Consulate-General, Amalienstraße 62, Munich 40, Tel. 39 40 15.

Libraries are available at the British Council (Bruderstraße 7, Tel. 22 33 26) and the Amerika-Haus (Karolinenplatz 3, Tel. 59 53 69).

Church services in English: American Episcopal (Anglican), Emmauskirche, Langobardenstraße 16, Sun. 11.30.

Baptist, Holzstraße 9, Munich 5, Sun. 11.45.

Accommodation in Munich

Visitors are recommended to book accommodation in advance, particularly in the summer months, during the Oktoberfest, or in Fasching (the carnival season). A single room costs between 35 and 193 DM, according to hotel category; a double room costs 40 to 306 DM.

Luxury Hotels

Bayerischer Hof, Promenadeplatz 2–6, Tel. 2 12 00, reservation 2 12 09 00-9 03. Continental, Max-Joseph-Straße 5, Tel. 55 79 71. Der Königshof, Karlsplatz 25, Tel. 55 84 12. Hilton, Am Tucherpark 7, Tel. 34 00 51. Sheraton, Arabellastraße 6, Tel. 92 40 11. Vier Jahreszeiten-Kempenski, Maximilianstraße 17, Tel. 22 88 21.

First Class Hotels

Arabella-Hotel, Arabellastraße 5, Tel. 9 23 21. Crest Hotel München, Effnerstraße 99, Tel. 98 25 41. Deutscher Kaiser, Arnulfstraße 2, Tel. 55 83 21. Eden-Hotel-Wolff, Arnulfstraße 4–8, Tel. 55 82 81. Excelsior, Schützenstraße 11, Tel. 55 79 06. Holiday Inn, Leopoldstraße 200, Tel. 34 09 71. International Hotel Auer, Hohenzollernstraße 5, Tel. 33 30 43. Olympiapark-Hotel, Helene-Mayer-Ring 12, Tel. 3 51 60 71. Penta, Hochstraße 3, Tel. 4 48 55 55. Residence, Arthur-Kutscher-Platz 4, Tel. 39 90 41. Tourotel, Domagkstraße 26, Tel. 38 10 00.

Good Hotels

Ambassador, Mozartstraße 4, Tel. 53 08 40. An der Oper, Falkenturmstraße 10, Tel. 22 87 11. Ariston (garni), Unsöldstraße 10, Tel. 22 26 91, Bräupfanne, Oberföhringer Straße 107a, Tel. 95 10 95, Bundesbahnhotel, im Hauptbahnhof, Tel. 55 85 71. Drei Löwen, Schillerstraße 8, Tel. 59 55 21. Europäischer Hof, Bayerstraße 31, Tel. 55 46 21. Germania, Schwanthalerstraße 28, Tel. 59 77 03. Haberstock, Schillerstraße 4, Tel. 55 78 55. Königswache, Steinheilstraße 7, Tel. 52 20 01. Leopold, Leopoldstraße 119, Tel. 36 70 61, Mark, Senefelderstraße 12, Tel. 59 28 01. Metropol, Bayerstraße 43, Tel. 53 07 64. Präsident, Lindwurmstraße 13, Tel. 26 30 11. Schweizerhof, Goethestraße 26, Tel. 53 96 31. Splendid (garni), Maximilianstraße 54, Tel. 29 66 06.

Inexpensive Hotels

Alfa (garni), Hirtenstraße 22, Tel. 95 23 77. Amba (garni), Arnulfstraße 20, Tel. 59 29 21. Blauer Bock (garni), Blumenstraße 16, Tel. 24 10 71. Dachs (garni), Amalienstraße 12, Tel. 28 80 86. Daniel (garni), Sonnenstraße 5, Tel. 55 49 45, Kraft (garni), Schillerstraße 49, Tel. 59 48 23. Vitalis, Kathi-Kobus-Straße 24, Tel. 18 00 11 (Motel).

Boarding Houses

There are boarding houses in all parts of the city. Single rooms cost between 25 and 45 DM. The tourist office (Tel. 2 39 12 55-2 60) will supply information.

Youth Accommodation

Jugendherberge München, Wendl-Dietrich-Straße 30, München 19, Tel. 13 11 56. Jugendgästehaus Thalkirchen, Miesingstraße 4, München 70, Tel. 7 23 65 50. Haus International, Elisabethstraße 87, München 40, Tel. 18 50 81. Burg Schwaneck, Burgweg 4–6, 8023 Pullach, Tel. 7 93 23 81 (situated in the area of the S-Bahn). Jugendherberge im Jugendwohnheim Salesianum, Wolfgangplatz 10, München 80, Tel. 4 13 83 30. Jugendgästehaus des CVJM, Landwehrstraße 13, München 2, Tel. 55 59 41. Jugendhotel für weibliche Jugendliche (youth hotel for girls), Goethestraße 9, München 2, Tel. 55 58 91.
For further information refer to youth information centre, Tel. 53 16 55.

Camping

Thalkirchen, Zentralländstraße 49, Tel. 7 23 17 07. Open from the middle of March until the end of October.
Obermenzing, Lochhausener Straße 59, Tel. 8 11 22 35. Open throughout the year.
Langwieder See, Eschenriederstraße 119, Tel. 8 14 15 66. Open from Apr. 1st to Oct. 15th.
Ludwigsfeld, Dachauer Straße 571, Tel. 1 50 37 90. Open throughout the year.
Ampersee, 8031 Geiselbullach, Tel. (0 81 42) 1 27 86. Open from May 1st to Oct. 30th.
Jugendlager Kapuzinerhölzl, near Franz-Schrank-Straße, Tel. 1 41 43 00. Open from the end of June until the beginning of September.

Food and Drink

"Food and drink keep body and soul together." This sentence expresses the Bavarian baroque joy of life. The Munich cuisine is based on the cuisine of Upper Bavaria. Influences from Tyrol, Bohemia, Franconia, Swabia, and especially from Italy are traceable.

Specialities

A magic word for Munich cooking is "Brotzeit". It can be taken at any hour of the day and is best translated with the word "snack". A Brotzeit can consists of:

Leberkäs: It contains neither liver nor is it any kind of cheese. This baked mixture of minced beef and pork, along with various spices like marjoram and nutmeg can be eaten hot or cold.

Weißwürste: White sausages are made out of veal, bacon and parsley. They are spiced with sweet mustard and eaten with "Laugenbrezen", hard crusty bread twists. Weißwürste are not allowed to hear the bell strike 12 o'clock, i.e. they should be eaten only before noon.

Wurstsalat: Slices of a particular kind of cold sausage (Leoner) with a lot of onion rings, vinegar, oil and pepper.

Radi: This white radish is cut in thin slices and salted; then one should wait a few minutes while the radish is "crying", which takes away its hot flavour.

Obatzter: Cheese, mostly Camembert mixed with minced onions, pepper, salt, paprika, caraway, yolk and butter; sometimes Gervais is used as the basic ingredient.

Old Munich Restaurants

Altes Hackerhaus, Sendlinger Straße 75.

Augustinerbräu, Neuhauser Straße 16.

Donisl, Weinstraße 1, am Marienplatz.

Franziskaner, Perusastraße 5.

Hackerkeller, Theresienhöhe 4.

Haxnbauer, Münzstraße 5.

Hofbräuhaus, Am Platzl 9.

Hundskugel, Hotterstraße 18 (oldest inn in Munich, dating from 1440).

Mathäser Bierstadt, Bayerstraße 5.

Max-Emanuel-Brauerei (garden), Adalbertstraße 33.

Nürnberger Bratwurstglöckl, am Dom.

Peterhof, Marienplatz 22.

Ratskeller, im Rathaus.

Schloßwirtschaft zur Schwaige (garden), Schloß Nymphenburg 30.

Spatenhaus, Residenzstraße 12.

Spöckmeier, Rosenstraße 9.

St. Emmeramsmühle (garden), St. Emmeram 41.

Torggelstuben, Am Platzl 6–8.

Weichandhof (garden), Obermenzing, Betzenweg 81.

Zum Bögner, Im Tal 72.

First-class Restaurants

Aubergine, Maximiliansplatz 5.

Boettner, Theatinerstraße 8.

Käferschänke, Schumannstraße 1.

Le Gourmet, Ligsalzstraße 46.

Sabitzer, Reitmorstraße 21.

Schwarzwälder, Hartmannstraße 8 (old Munich wine restaurant).

Tantris, Johann-Fichte-Straße 7.

Walterspiel, Maximilianstraße 17.

Speciality Restaurants

French:

Aquitaine, Amalienstraße 39.

Bouillabaisse, Falkenturmstraße 10.

La Belle Epoque, Maximilianstraße 29.

La Mer, Schraudolphstraße 24.

Le Bazar, Bauerstraße 2.

Werneckhof, Werneckstraße 11.

Italian:

Bei Milan, Weinstraße 7.

Da Pipo, Brahmsstraße 32.

El Toula, Sparkassenstraße 5.

Osteria Italiana, Schellingstraße 62.

Romagna Antica, Elisabethstraße 52.

Tivoli, Widenmayerstraße 52.

Other:

Canton (Chinese), Theresienstraße 49.

Churrasco (steaks), Nikolaistraße 9.

Costa (Greek), Barer Straße 42.

Daitokai (Japanese), Kurfürstenstraße 57.

Hofbräuhaus

Datscha (Turkmenian), Kaiserstraße 3.

Goldene Stadt (Bohemian), Oberanger 44.

Mifune (Japanese), Ismaninger Straße 136.

Opatija (Yugoslavian), Rindermarkt 2.

Palenque (Mexican), Mauerkircher-straße 2.

Piroschka (Hungarian), in Haus der Kunst.

Schwabinger Grillroom (steaks), Georgenstraße 26.

Sultana (Indian), Franz-Joseph-Str. 28.

Tai Tung (Chinese), Prinzregentenstraße 60.

Trader Vic's (Polynesian), Promenade-platz 4 (in Bayerischer Hof).

Munich Beer

The main drink in Munich and through-out Bavaria is still beer. Protected by the oldest food law, Duke William's "purity injunction" of 1516, which forbids the use of anything but water, barley and hops in brewing, Bavarian beer is still made from natural product without any addition of chemical.

The light and dark draught beer (lager) has a wort of 11–12 per cent, "Märzen-bier" has 13–14 per cent. During certain times of the year "Bock" beer is brewed, with a wort of 18–19 per cent. A special kind of beer is "Weißbier" (white beer), a light, slightly sparkling beer made from wheat instead of barley. Since 1977 the Bavarian "Alt" beer has been brewed again.

The measure for beer is the "Maß" which is about one litre, half of this is "eine Halbe", a quarter is called a "Quartel" or "ein Schoppen".

Beer Gardens

Augustinerkeller, Arnulfstraße 52.

Aumeister, Sondermeierstraße 1.

Brauereischänke Aying, Münchner Straße 2, Aying.

Brückenwirt, An der Brücke 1, Höll-riegelskreuth.

Chinesischer Turm, im Engl. Garten.

Hirschau, Gyßlingstraße 7, im Engl. Garten.

Hirschgarten, Hirschgartenstraße 1.

Hofbräu-Keller, Innere Wiener Str. 19.

Kloster Andechs (only open until 8 p.m.), near Herrsching.

Kloster Schäftlarn (open until 10 p.m.).

Kreitmair, Keferloh 13.

Löwenbräu-Keller, Stiglmaierplatz.

Osterwaldgarten, Keferstraße 12.

Pschorr-Keller, Theresienhöhe 7.

Salvatorkeller, Hochstraße 77.

Sankt Emmeramsmühle, Sankt Emmeram 41.

Wine Houses

Badische Weinstuben, Marsstraße 5.

Feldherrnkeller, Theatinerstraße 27.

Hahnhof (7 in Munich).

Neuner, Herzogspitalstraße 8.

Palais-Keller, Promenadeplatz 2.

Pfälzer Probierstuben, Residenzstraße 1.

Pfälzer Weinkeller, Frauenplatz 11.

Schneider, Sparkassenstraße 1.

Schwarzwälder, Hartmannstraße 2.

Weinstadl (the oldest house in Munich), Burgstraße 5.

Weinkrüger, Maximilianstraße 21 and Feilitzschstraße 25.

Student Restaurants

Alter Simpl, Türkenstraße 57.

Atzinger, Schellingstraße 9.

Bauernwirt, Clemensstraße 7.

Café an der Uni, Ludwigstraße.

Die Palme, Zentnerstraße 13.

Haus der 111 Biere, Franzstraße 3.

Occampils, Occamstraße 11.

Schwabinger Spritz'n, Hesseloher Straße 20.

Uhu, Theresienstraße 138.

Weinbauer, Fendstraße 5.

Shopping

As a city of art, fashion and fair, Munich of course has a wide range of shops, which provide a choice of goods to suit every taste and wallet.

Fashion

Munich bears with pride the attributes of a city of fashion. Some of the world's most elegant fashion houses have their branch stores in Munich. Not only the most extravagant new trends but also Bavarian folk costumes are to be seen – especially in the attractive boutiques of Schwabing.

For the particularly fastidious taste the fashion shops of Maximilianstraße are recommended. Bagheera, Courrèges, TAP, Guy Laroche, Lothar's and St. Laurent, among others, have branch stores there. But there are also old-established fashion stores like English House, Rudolph Moshammer, or Unützer, which are dominated by elegant and sporty outfits.

Genuine elegance is offered in Theatinerstraße (Eckerle-Moden, Maendler, Rodier), in Perusastraße (Otto Weller), in Residenzstraße (Max Dietl, Daniel Hechter, Ponater-Modelle), in Brienner Straße (E. Braun), at Amiraplatz (Ted Lapidus, Missoni) and at Promenadeplatz (Rudolph Moshammer, Emilio Pucci). Loden-Frey is situated in Maffeistraße.

Lower-priced stores are at Marienplatz (Beck), in Rosenstraße (Fischer), in Kaufingerstraße (Arendt), in Neuhauser Straße (Stalf, Haus der Mode, Lacher), as well as in Sendlinger Straße.

Big department stores are located mainly in the pedestrian zones (Kaufinger-, Neuhauser-, and Schützenstraße), and at Karlsplatz.

Boutiques can be found especially in Schwabing in Türkenstraße, Amalienstraße, Leopoldstraße, and Hohenzollernstraße.

Shoe stores for elegant and extravagant tastes are located in Theatiner-, Perusa- and Maximilianstraße. Lower-priced stores are in Kaufinger- and Neuhauser Straße.

Men's and women's clothes in the Bavarian style can be purchased at Loden-Frey (Maffeistraße, the largest special store for loden cloth and national costume in the world), Dirndl-Königin (Residenzstraße), Wallach (Residenzstraße), Die schöne Münchnerin (Peterplatz), Salzburger Trachtenstube (Neuhauser Straße), Trachtenalm (Herzogspitalstraße) and at Zugspitz-Moden (Bahnhofsplatz, Neuhauser and Sendlinger Straße).

Art shops

The art trade is concentrated in Maximilianstraße, in Brienner- and Theatinerstraße, and also in many smaller galeries in the arcades of the Hofgarten and in Schwabing (Türkenstraße).

Antiques

Valuable (and expensive) antiques are offered in the shops of Fürstenstraße. All over Schwabing (especially in Barer- and Türkenstraße) there are shops specializing in "English antiques", silver, glass, Jugendstil (Art Nouveau), or Art Deco. At Antic-Haus (Neuturmstraße 1) several dealers have set up a mutual undertaking in a huge area. In addition, there are many smaller antique shops grouped around Viktualienmarkt. Haimhausen Palace near Dachau is a meeting place for collectors of exquisite antiques. Every year in autumn the *German Art and Antic Fair* takes place at the Haus der Kunst. In addition, there are several smaller antique fairs at the Deutsches Museum and the Pschorr-Keller.

Furnishings and Arts and Crafts

Furnishing of quality is offered by stores in Brienner Straße (Beringer und Koettgen, Vereinigte Werkstätten). The big furniture stores are located in the Tal. Haus Bernheimer at Lenbachplatz specializes in furnishings, art, and antiques. The Kunstgewerbe-Verein in Pacellistraße is known for arts and crafts, in particular Bavarian articles, but there are also numerous shops in Theatiner- and Maximilianstraße.

Bookshops

As a great publishing city Munich has a wide variety of bookshops, especially in the central city.

English books can be bought at Anglia, Schellingstraße 3.

Evening Entertainment

Opera

Nationaltheater, Max-Joseph-Platz. Advance booking only at Maximilianstraße 11. (Tel. 22 13 16) from Mon. to Fri. 10 a.m.−12.30 p.m. and 3.30−5.30 p.m. Also at the ticket window of the opera one hour before performance.

Operetta

Staatstheater am Gärtnerplatz, Gärtnerplatz 3 (Tel. 2 60 32 32). Advance booking Mon.−Fri. 10 a.m.−12.30 p.m. and 3.30−5.30 p.m., Sat. 10 a.m.−12.30 p.m. Also at the theatre ticket window one hour before performance. In addition to popular operettas and musicals, operas are also performed here.

Theatres

Altes Residenztheater (Cuvilliéstheater), in the Residence. Entrance Residenzstraße (Tel. 22 13 16). Advance booking as with Nationaltheater. Operas and plays suitable to this most beautiful rococo theatre in the world are performed here, also Lieder matinées and chamber music concerts.

Residenztheater, Max-Joseph-Platz 1 (Tel. 2 18 54 13 or 22 57 54). Advance booking Mon.−Fri. 10 a.m.−12.30 p.m. and 3.30−5.30 p.m., Sat. 10 a.m.−12 p.m. Box office one hour before performance. Classical and modern dramas.

Münchner Kammerspiele, in the Schauspielhaus, Maximilianstraße 26 (Tel. 22 43 38). Advance booking Mon.−Fri. 10 a.m.−6 p.m., Sat., Sun. and holidays 10 a.m.−1 p.m. Classical and modern dramas.

Theater im Marstall, Marstallplatz (Tel. 22 57 54). For advance booking see Nationaltheater. Experimental performances of the State Opera and the Residenztheater.

Werkraumtheater der Münchner Kammerspiele, Hildegardstraße 1 (Tel. 22 43 38). Advance booking as in Kammerspiele. Experimental stage for avantgarde theatre.

Kleine Komödie, in the Bayerischer Hof, Promenadeplatz (Tel. 29 28 10) and at Max-II-Monument (Tel. 22 18 54). Advance booking Mon.−Sat. 11 a.m.−7 p.m., Sun. 3−7 p.m. Boulevard and popular theatre.

T(h)eater Brienner Straße, Brienner Straße 50 (Tel. 52 19 07). Advance booking Mon.−Sat. 11 a.m.−7 p.m. Boulevard plays and guest performances.

Theater "Kleine Freiheit", Maximilianstraße 31 (Tel. 22 11 23). Advance booking Mon.−Sat. as of 11 a.m., Sun. as of 2 p.m. until performance. Boulevard theatre with famous actors.

Piccola Bavaria, Theater im Künstlerhaus, Lenbachplatz 8 (Tel. 59 80 36). Advance booking daily as of 11 a.m. Avant-garde theatre.

Modernes Theater, Hans-Sachs-Straße 12 (Tel. 26 68 21). Advance booking (Tel. 22 54 73) daily except Mon. 4−6.30 p.m. Avant-garde theatre.

Off-Off, Theatre Club, Potsdamer Straße 13. Advance booking as of 6 p.m. (Tel. 39 37 29). Avant-garde theatre, performances Thurs.−Sun.

Theater rechts der Isar, Wörthstraße 9. Advance booking by telephone 10 a.m.−1 p.m. (Tel. 8 34 91 38) and as of 4 p.m. (Tel. 4 48 36 57). Modern plays.

Theater über dem Landtag, Maria-Theresia-Straße 2a. Advance booking as of 4 p.m. (Tel. 47 91 18), daily except Mon. Modern drama.

Theater am Einlaß, Am Einlaß 4 (Tel. 2 60 82 80). Advance booking 10 a.m.−12 noon and 6−8 p.m., daily except Sun. Works by modern dramatists.

Theater 44, Hohenzollernstraße 20. Advance booking by telephone as of 4 p.m. (Tel. 32 87 48), daily except Mon. Modern drama.

Theater am Sozialamt, Haimhauser Straße 13a. Advance booking by telephone as of 3 p.m. (Tel. 34 58 90), daily except Sun. and Mon. Modern plays, sometimes in dialect.

Theater k, Kurfürstenstraße 8 (Tel. 33 39 33). Advance booking as of 4 p.m., daily except Mon. and Tues. Experimental theatre.

Bliss-Theater, Guldeinstraße 47. Advance booking by telephone 2−7 p.m. (Tel. 50 85 86). Texts, lyrics, chamber music.

pro T, Isabellastraße 40. Advance booking by telephone (Tel. 4 48 66 93 and 2 71 41 62) Wed.−Sat. Avant-garde theatre.

Deutsches Theater, Schwanthalerstraße 13 (Tel. 59 34 27). Advance booking Mon.–Sat. 10 a.m. – 6 p.m., Son. 2 – 7 p.m. Revues, musicals. International guest performances.

Kleine Bühne Schwabing, Hesseloher Straße 3. Advance booking by telephone 34 96 90 as of 3 p.m., ticket office as of 6 p.m., daily except Sun. and Mon. Contemporary theatre, popular plays, songs, and ballads.

studiotheater, Ungererstraße 19. Advance booking daily as of 11 a.m. (Tel. 34 38 27 and 34 38 86). Modern drama.

Bairisches Raritätentheater, in Rheinhof, Bayerstraße 27 (Tel. 55 51 70). Advance booking as of 11 a.m., daily except Mon. Folk theatre in dialect.

Münchner Theater für Kinder, Dachauer Straße 46 (Tel. 59 54 54). Advance booking daily except Mon. 10 a.m. – 2 p.m.

Münchner Marionettentheater, Blumenstraße 29a (Tel. 26 57 12). Advance booking Wed.–Sat. 10 a.m. – 12 noon and 2–4.30 p.m., Sun. 11 a.m. – 3 p.m. Puppet theatre.

Cabarets

Münchner Lach- und Schießgesellschaft, Haimhauser/corner Ursulastraße (Tel. 39 19 97). Advance booking daily except Sun. as of 2 p.m. Political cabaret.

Münchner Rationaltheater, Hesseloher Straße 18 (Tel. 33 50 40 and 33 40 50). Advance booking daily except Monday as of 2 p.m. Political cabaret.

Scala Theater, in Drugstore, Feilitzschstraße (Tel. 33 50 40 and 33 40 50), Tues.– Sat. Cabaret.

Schwabinger Brettl, Occamstraße 11 (Tel. 34 72 89). Advance booking the day before as of 8 p.m. Admission free. Chansons, folklore.

Schwabinger Kleinkunstbühne "Heppel und Ettlich", Kaiserstraße 67 (Tel. 34 93 59), every Fri. and Sat. Reservation as of 6 p.m. Cabaret.

Drehleier, Balanstraße 23 (Tel. 48 43 37), Theatre, Varieté, Rock.

Platzl, Münzstraße 8–9 (Tel. 29 31 01), daily. Bavarian nonsense, cabaret.

Song Parnass, Einsteinstraße 42 (Tel. 4 70 29 95). Reservation as of 6 p.m., daily except Mon. Chansons, cabaret.

Liederbühne Robinson, Dreimühlenstraße 33 (Tel. 77 22 68), Thurs.–Sat. Cabaret, folklore.

Cinemas

There are numerous cinemas all over Munich. The main "art film" cinemas recommended are *Theatiner-Filmkunst* in Theatinerstraße, *Isabella* in Neureutherstraße, *Türkendolch* and *Neues Arri* in Türkenstraße, *Lupe 2* in Ungererstraße.

Concerts

Musical life, divided mainly between the *Herkulessaal*, the *Kongreßsaal* in the Deutsches Museum, the *Großer Sendesaal des Bayerischen Rundfunks* and the *Olympiahalle*, is rich in variety and number of performances. Munich has four large symphony orchestras: *Bayerisches Staatsorchester*, *Münchner Philharmoniker*, *Bayerisches Rundfunkorchester*, and *Symphonieorchester Graunke*. In addition to the *Münchner Kammerorchester*, there are also many other chamber music groups.

Monthly Programmes

For 1.30 DM the *Offizielles Monatsprogramm des Fremdenverkehrsamtes München* or the *Münchner Programm* can be purchased at almost every bookstore and kiosk. Both brochures provide information about all events and performances, as well as times, dates, and reservation possibilities.

Circus

Munich's famous *Circus Krone* owns the only permanent circus building in Germany (Marsstraße 43).

Night-clubs

Munich night life offers a wide variety of night-clubs with floor shows and various music programmes (Jazz, Pop, etc.). The following is only a selection:

Cabaret Eve (Striptease), in Reginahaus, Maximiliansplatz 5.

Charly M. (Disco), Maximiliansplatz 5.

Domicile (Jazz), Leopoldstraße 19.

East Side (Disco), Rosenheimer Str. 30.

Hanno's Piano Bar, Neureutherstr. 15.

Harry's New York Bar, Falkenturmstr. 9.

Lola Montez (Striptease), Am Platzl 1.

Memoland (Jazz), Siegesstraße 19.

Sugar Shack (Disco), Herzogspitalstr. 6.

Sunset (Disco), Leopoldstraße 69.

Transport

Public transport is amalgamated in the so-called *Münchner Verkehrs- und Tarifverbund*. This means that a properly stamped ticket (there are plans about ticket prices and distances at the train stations) is good for the immediate area on all S- and U-Bahnen (S-trains and subways) and also trams and buses. Normally public transport runs from 5 a.m. to 1 a.m. The S- and U-Bahn lines are listed in the following plan.

U-Bahn (Underground)

Line U 3: Holzapfelkreuth – Westpark – Partnachplatz – Harras – Implerstraße – Poccistraße – Goetheplatz – Sendlinger Tor – Marienplatz – Odeonsplatz – Universität – Giselastraße – Münchner Freiheit – Bonner Platz – Scheidplatz – Petuelring – Olympiazentrum.

Linie U 6: From Holzapfelkreuth to Münchner Freiheit like U 3, then Dietlindenstraße – Nordfriedhof – Alte Heide – Studentenstadt – Freimann – Kieferngarten.

Line U 8: Neuperlach Süd – Therese-Giese-Allee – Neuperlach Zentrum – Quiddestraße – Michaelibad – Innsbrucker Ring – Karl-Preis-Platz – Giesing – Untersbergstraße – Silberhornstraße – Kolumbusplatz – Fraunhoferstraße – Sendlinger Tor – Hauptbahnhof – Königsplatz – Theresienstraße – Josephsplatz – Hohenzollernplatz – Scheidplatz – Petuelring – Olympiazentrum.

S-Bahn

The S-Bahn, which is operated by the federal railway, joins Munich to the region around the city. Connections with other means of public transport at junctions on the uniform main line: Laim – Donnersberger Brücke – Hackerbrücke – Hauptbahnhof – Karlsplatz – Marienplatz – Isartor – Rosenheimer Platz – Ostbahnhof.

S 1: Freising – Oberschleißheim – Moosach – main line – Giesing – Aying – Kreuzstraße.

S 2: Petershausen – Dachau – Allach – main line – Giesing – Deisenhofen – Holzkirchen.

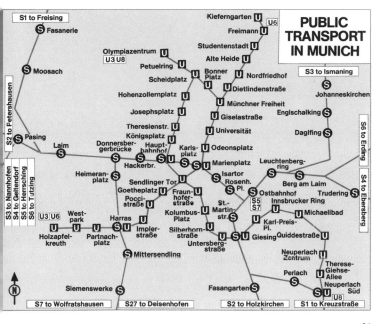

21

S 3: Nannhofen – Maisach – Pasing – main line – Johanneskirchen – Ismaning.
S 4: Geltendorf – Fürstenfeldbruck – Pasing – main line – Berg am Laim – Zorneding – Ebersberg.
S 5: Herrsching – Unterpfaffenhofen – Pasing – main line – Ostbahnhof.
S 6: Tutzing – Starnberg – Gauting – Pasing – main line – Riem – Erding.
S 7: Wolfratshausen – Hohenschäftlarn – Harras – Hauptbahnhof – Ostbahnhof.
S 12: Pasing – Harras – Deisenhofen.
S 27: Hauptbahnhof (Starnberger Bahnhof) – Harras – Solln – Deisenhofen.

Trams

This is a list of the most important tram routes:

12: Harthof – Scheidplatz – Nordbad – Leonrodplatz – Rotkreuzplatz – Romanplatz – Amalienburgstraße.
15: Sendlinger Tor – Mariahilfplatz (Auer Dult) – Großhesseloher Brücke.
16: – Harras – Fürstenried.
18: Petuelring – Nordbad – Hohenzollernplatz – Barer Straße – Karlsplatz – Sendlinger Tor – Isartor – Deutsches Museum – Effnerplatz.
19: Pasing – Laim – Hauptbahnhof – Karlsplatz – Maximilianstraße – Steinhausen.
20: Moosach – Stiglmaierplatz – Hauptbahnhof – Karlsplatz – Sendlinger Tor – Deutsches Museum – Effnerplatz.
25: Sendlinger Tor – Mariahilfplatz (Auer Dult) – Großhesseloher Brücke – Grünwald.
27: Harras – Messegelände (West) – Hauptbahnhof – Karlsplatz – Ostfriedhof – Schwanseestraße.
29: Willibaldplatz – Trappentreustraße – Karlsplatz – Sendlinger Tor.

Buses

The most important routes are:

31: Thalkirchen (Tierpark) – Implerstraße – Laim (Bahnhof).
32: Harras – Messegelände – Rotkreuzplatz.
33: Münchner Freiheit – Nordbad – Rotkreuzplatz – Donnersberger Brücke – Ratzingerplatz.
52: Marienplatz – Alemannenstraße (Tierpark).
57: Sendlinger Tor – Thalkirchen (Tierpark).
73: Amalienburgstraße – Pasing.
91: Steinhausen – Flughafen Riem.

Fares

For people taking more than four rides per day with public transport, the 24 hours ticket is highly recommended.

The "blue" 24 hours ticket for 6 DM (children 2 DM) is valid for the extended city area and is sufficient for visits to the important sights.

The "green" 24 hours ticket for 10 DM (children 4 DM) is advisable for visits to Freising, Starnberg, Schleißheim, or Dachau. This ticket is valid for the whole public transport area.

For visitors of Munich who do not need a 24 hours ticket: The public transport area is divided into zones and fare stages, which are described on plans at every stop. In the extended city area a ride with a single-journey ticket costs 2 DM. The same ride costs 1.67 DM with a multiple-journey ticket (at least two stripes per ride must be stamped here). Short trips (within two fare stages) costs 1.50 DM with a single-journey ticket, 1.22 DM with a multiple-journey ticket. Children from 4 to 15 must pay 0.70 DM in the city area for a single-journey ticket, 0.56 DM for a multiple-journey ticket (a "red K", on which only one stripe per ride must be stamped). All tickets can be purchased from machines at larger stops. Multiple-journey tickets are also available at ticket machines in the rear wagons of trams. Single-journey tickets can be bought from the tram and bus driver (bus drivers also provide the regular blue multiple-journey ticket). Prices will probably rise at 1984.

Taxi

Taxi stands are to be found all over Munich. If you want to call a taxi, it is advisable to have a look at the inside front cover of the telephone book, where the various numbers for the city are listed according to regions. Advanced bookings only with telephone numbers 26 70 77 and 26 70 78. The beginning charge is 2.70 DM, every kilometre 1.50 DM (outside the city limit 1.70 DM).

The inexpensive Call-Cars and Mini-Cars do not pick up passengers on the street, but can only be booked by telephone (55 53 33, 55 54 44 and 55 83 83).

Airport

Buses to the airport leave from Hauptbahnhof-Nordseite (north side of the main railway station in the Arnulfstraße) every 20 min. from 5.40 a.m. to 8.40 p.m.

The walk described below covers Munich's main artery: the main shopping and business centre. About 2 hours are needed for viewing this area in detail.

Karlsplatz [1]

The townspeople call this square "Stachus", which is probably an abbreviation of the Christian name of *Eustachius Föderl*, who, from 1726 onwards, had a shooting inn here, just outside the city walls, which were then still standing. Karlsplatz was laid out in 1791, when Elector Karl Theodor (1777–1799) ordered the city's fortifications to be torn down at various points and the moat filled in. Today there is a four-storey subterranean shopping centre with modern shops in the upper storey. Karlsplatz is an important transport junction. It is only 5 minutes by foot from the main railway station and 15 minutes from Marienplatz.

On the north of the square is the *Justizpalast* (Palace of Justice or law courts), built in 1891–1897 by Friedrich Thiersch in late Renaissance style. On the east side there is the only closed part of the square, consisting of a semi-circle of buildings, in the middle of which – behind a modern fountain – is the

Karlstor

This structure was the former west gate inside the second city fortification under Ludwig the Bavarian (1314–1347) and was called Neuhauser Tor. The towers standing today were rebuilt by Rumford when Elector Karl Theodor had the square laid out. A vast pedestrian zone, constructed in 1966, extends along *Neuhauser Straße* and *Kaufinger Straße*.

Bürgersaal [2]

In 1709–1710 "St. Mary's Congregation of Lords and Citizens on the occasion of the Annunciation to our beloved Lady" had this "assembly hall" constructed. It was built by Georg Ettenhofer according to the plans of Giovanni Antonio Viscardi. This two-storey church was almost totally destroyed in 1944 by bombs; only the main façade remaining undamaged.

The main room, the decoration of which was entrusted to Johann Georg Bader (wall pieces) and Johann Anton Gumpp (frescoes) in the 18th century, has been restored like the old Bürgersaal; between 1971 and 1980 stucco, wall and ceiling frescoes were created anew. On the side walls are 14 murals in oil by Franz Joachim Beich (1719), which depict the most famous Bavarian pilgrimages. From Andreas Faistenberger's important high altar (1710) the war spared only the

Karlstor

relief of the Annunciation. The *Guardian Angel group* (1763) is one of Ignaz Günther's masterpieces. The same artist created designs for the silver busts on the Mensa, which were made by Joseph Heinrich Kanzler in 1776.

On the ground floor, kept in almost total darkness, since 1948 is the grave of the Munich Jesuit priest *Rupert Mayer* (d. 1945), who was persecuted during the Third Reich.

Alte Akademie [3]

The noble and restrained façade of the Old Academy, the *former Jesuit college* (Neuhauser Straße 51) was built by Friedrich Sustris from 1585 to 1597. Duke Wilhelm V encouraged the Jesuits, who had come to Munich in 1559, because he regarded them the most potent weapon of the Counterreformation. After the dissolution of the Jesuit Order (in 1773 by Pope Clement XIV), the college was used, in turn, as the seat for the Academy of Sciences, the University (1826–1840), the State Library (until 1843), the Academy of Fine Arts (until 1885) and the Bavarian Office of Statistics. – The *Richard Strauss Fountain*, with its figure group from the opera "Salome" at the little square here, was designed by Hans Wimmer in remembrance of Munich's famous son, the composer of world-known operas.

23

Duke Wilhelm V was also the founder of the nearby

*Michaelskirche [4]

The construction of St. Michael's church began in 1583. After the tower collapsed (1590), also causing damage to the choir section, the duke entrusted the Dutchman Friedrich Sustris with the completion of the church. Sustris, along with Wendel Dietrich, had already worked on the original construction under the direction of Wolfgang Müller. In 1597 the official dedication of the church took place. In the Second World War the church was seriously damaged. Rebuilding began in the years 1946/47.

The impressive *façade* was restored in 1972. Between the two portals there is a large niche with the *bronze figure of the archangel Michael,* who triumphs over evil, which is depicted in the form of a dragon. The figure was modelled by Hubert Gerhard, the casting was made by Martin Frey (1592). In the other smaller niches of the upper stories and the gable stand the founder Wilhelm V (first storey, third from the right with the model church) and his Wittelsbach ancestors. The highest niche is reserved for Christ the Saviour.

The *interior* was regarded at the time as an architectural sensation. Up to this point people were only familiar with the high-pillared Gothic naves, but now a gigantic Renaissance hall, 20 metres wide and with a *barrel vault ceiling,* opened up before the eyes of the believers. At the time only St. Peter's Cathedral in Rome had larger dimensions. The stucco decorations of the partitioned barrel vault (Hubert Gerhard), which was destroyed in the war, were restored in 1981. The *high altar* was erected by Wendel Dietrich between 1586 and 1589. The altar-

piece was created by Christoph Schwarz (1587). The four bronze reliefs are by Hubert Gerhard (about 1595). In the left transept is the *tomb of Duke Eugen von Leuchtenberg* (Eugène de Beauharnais

St. Michael's and Frauenkirche

was the step son of Napoleon I and son-in-law of Max I Joseph), which was erected by Bertel Thorvaldsen in 1830. In the right transept is the cross monument by Giovanni da Bologna. The *Martyrdom of St. Ursula* and the *Annunciation to Mary* in the side chapel next to the transept were made by Peter Candid. Duke Wilhelm V, Elector Maximilian I and King Ludwig II are buried in the *vault* under the choir.

On the corner of Neuhauser Straße and Augustinerstraße, we come to an impres-

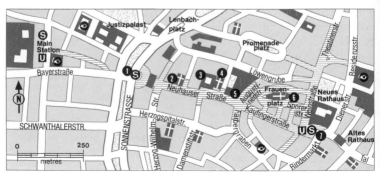

sive building, which is essentially a Gothic survival:

The former Augustinerkirche [5]

Between 1291 and 1294 the Augustinian Hermit-Friars built a church and monastery at this place then still outside the city walls constructed by Henry the Lion. The church was greatly altered in the 14th, 15th, and 17th centuries. After the monastery was dissolved in 1803 the church was secularized, the hall being used as an office for tolls. Where the former monastery used to be are the present day police headquarters. In 1911 construction of shops on the ground floor of the basilica began. Since 1966 the church has served as the *Deutsches Jagd- und Fischereimuseum* (German Hunting and Fishing Museum) with collections of hunting weapons, trophies, paintings and drawings, splendid hunting sledges and a fishing section. Among the curiosities are the collection of documents concerning the story of the poacher Bayerischer Hiasl and the legendary Wolpertinger.

Opposite the church, on the corner of the building where the clothing store Hirmer is located, is a little *stone figure* with the model of a tower. The model is a representation of the Schöner Turm ("beautiful tower"), which stood here until 1807 as part of the western boundary of Henry the Lion's Munich. The curve of the *Augustinerstraße* follows the line of the oldest city wall. Going along this street one soon reaches *Frauenplatz,* passes the granite-block fountain built by Bernhard Winkler in 1972 and is confronted by the west façade of the

**Frauenkirche [6]

Its official name is *Dom und Stadtpfarr- kirche zu Unserer Lieben Frau* (Cathedral and Parish Church of Our Beloved Lady). In 1468 the foundation of the cathedral was laid, after the Romanesque Marienkirche with its three naves (dating from 1271) was torn down. The earlier church had replaced the old chapel of the Virgin, of uncertain date, which had been built before the founding of Munich. *Jörg von Halspach,* called *Ganghofer,* was entrusted with the construction of the cathedral. The vault was already finished in 1477, the twin towers in 1488. The cupolas of the towers (100 and 99 m high resp.), which have become Munich's symbol, were not added until 1525. After the formation of the archbishopric of Munich and Freising (1821), the Frauenkirche became the cathedral.

The general design of the *main portal,* as well as that of the other four doors, was by Ignaz Günther (1772); the sculptures of Christ and Madonna with child on the side pedestrals are from the Romanesque basilica. The pedestal figures of Christ and Mary at the *Benno-Portal* date from the 15th century. The figure of St. Sebastian is by Andreas Faistenberger. The figures of Christ and Mary at the *Bride's Portal* go back to 1430.

The interior consists of a nave and two aisles, all of equal height (31 m), covered by a light yellow net vault (restored in 1980/81). There is not much left over from the war of the earlier elaborate decorations. Several of the remaining *Gothic stained-glass windows* deserve to be mentioned: the Annunciation to Mary (1392), the Scharfzandt Window (made by Peter Hemmel from Andlau in 1493) and the Three Magi Window, which depicts the life of Jesus of Nazareth (1430). These windows are located in the choir gallery. The choir stall was built anew in 1972. Of special interest are the *figures of the Apostles and Prophets* by Erasmus Grasser (1502) over the choir stall. The cathedral cross in the central nave was designed by Josef Henselmann in 1954. The pulpit is the work of Blasius Spreng (1957). The *wooden statue of St. Christopher* in the west part was made by an anonymous artist about 1520, the *bas- relief Mourning of Christ* was by Hans Krumper (1618).

At the west end of the southern side aisle is the **tomb monument of Emperor Ludwig the Bavarian.* Maximilian I entrusted Hans Krumper with the project of the "Castrum doloris" in black marble. Krumper also created the bronze figures of Albrecht V and Wilhelm IV, while Hubert Gerhard designed the four guard figures.

Behind the choir some steps lead down to the *Princes' Vault,* the resting place of the Wittelsbach rulers from the sons of Ludwig the Bavarian to Albrecht V. The last Bavarian king, Ludwig III, is also buried here. A second vault is reserved for the archbishops of Munich and Freising. – The south tower of the Frauenkirche has an elevator.

Sporerstraße brings us to Weinstraße and

*Marienplatz [7]

This square has been the urban centre of Munich since the foundation of the city in 1158. It has been called Marienplatz since 1854; before that the name was Schrannenplatz – a square for farmers to sell their products.

Neues Rathaus

The entire north side of Marienplatz is taken up by the Neues Rathaus (New Town Hall), which was constructed between 1867 and 1908 according to plans of Georg Haubenrisser. The main façade is adorned with figures representing Bavarian kings, electors, Munich "originals", and characters from allegory and legend.

The 85 metre *Rathaus tower* dominates the scene, with the fourth largest *Glokkenspiel* (chime) in Europe. 43 bells covering 3½ octaves play four different tunes *(daily at 11 a.m., in summer also at 5 p.m.).*

While the music is playing, two scenes with moving figures are portrayed: a remembrance of the victorious *tournament* at the marriage of the Bavarian Duke Wilhelm V and Renate of Lorraine in 1568 and the *Schäfflertanz,* a reminder of the dance by the coopers' guild in 1517, which gave the plague-ridden Munich new courage to live. All year round there is an evening performance at 9 p.m.: the "Münchner Kindl" (made in copper by Anton Schmidt in 1905) is put to bed by the Angel of Peace, after a nightwatchman with horn and lantern has given the signal.

*Mariensäule

Elector Maximilian I had the Virgin's Column erected in 1638 at Schrannenplatz as a memorial for the saving of the cities Munich and Landshut from the ravages of the Thirty Years' War. A monolith of red Tegernsee marble bears the 2.15 metre-high *Madonna figure.* The gilded statue with sceptre and crown stands on a crescent moon, along with the Christ child delivering a blessing. It is a work of Herbert Gerhard, who designed it in 1594 for the Frauenkirche, the high altar of which the statue graced until 1613. Four early baroque *putti,* symbolically fighting against the curses of mankind (plague, war, hunger and heresy), are decorations at the base of the column. The bronzes were probably made by Jörg Petel from Weilheim.

The *Fischbrunnen* (fish fountain) in the northeast corner of the square was erected in 1862–1865 by Konrad Knoll; it suffered severe damage in 1944 and was

built anew in 1954 by Josef Henselmann, who used some of the original bronze parts that had been saved.

Altes Rathaus

The east side of Marienplatz is limited by the Old Town Hall. The present building was erected in the years 1953–1958; it is however based on the Gothic model de-

New Town Hall

stroyed during the war, which had been worked out by Jörg von Halspach, the architect of the Frauenkirche, between 1470 and 1480. In former times the *Gothic hall* served mainly for dancing. It was considerell the most perfect late Gothic secular room in southern Germany. It has been restored in greatly simplified form. Erasmus Grasser created the sequence of 16 Moriskentänzer (Moresque dancers), of which unfortunately only ten have been preserved. Today they are on display in the Munich Stadtmuseum.

The former *Talbrucktor* (gateway), which spanned the remaining part of the street next to the town hall was rebuilt in 1972 by Erwin Schleich according to the Gothic original.

26

2nd Walk. The Burghers' Munich: St. Peter – Sendlinger Tor – Stadtmuseum – *Viktualienmarkt – Heiliggeistkirche

2

This walk can be undertaken as a continuation of the first walk. Without a visit to the Stadtmuseum it takes about 1½ hours.

Leaving Marienplatz we take the street *Rindermarkt* and after 100 m we reach the

Pfarrkirche St. Peter [8]

Even prior to the founding of the city by Henry the Lion, there had been a church with a barrel-vault from pre-Merovingian times on this site. This fact was revealed by excavations in the years 1952–1953. Already towards the end of the 12th century the second church in Bavarian Romanesque style was consecrated. After the church building had been expanded in Gothic style by order of the bishop of Freising and consecrated in 1294, it fell victim to the great fire of 1327 shortly thereafter. After its reconstruction St. Peter's was dedicated anew in 1368.

The *spire,* built anew in 1607 and rebuilt according to the original after the war, is regarded as one of Munich's landmarks. There is a great *view* of the city and the Alpine Foreland from its platform (*open on weekdays 9 a.m. – 5 p.m., Sun. 10 a.m. – 5 p.m. Admission charge*).

Many of the interior furnishings were preserved in the Second World War.

Most importantly, the *high altar* was rescued, to which Erasmus Grasser had contributed an enthroned figure of St. Peter (1492), Egid Quirin Asam the Four Fathers of the Church (1732) and Franz Schwanthaler two worshiping angels (1804). The figure of Christ and the statue of Mary on the right and left side of the altar are the work of Joseph Prötzner the Elder. The *five Gothic pictures* by Jan Polack (1517), which are now on the walls of the presbytery, used to be part of the high altar. Of further interest are the *Corporis-Christi-Altar* by Ignaz Günther (1758) on the front side of the northern aisle, the *Mariahilf-Altar* (1756, also by Günther) in the southern aisle, the *Aresinger-Epitaph* by Erasmus Grasser (1482) in the chapel under the north tower. The *St.-Eligius-Altar* is by Ignaz Günther as well (1770). The same artist created the *Epitaph of T. E. de Courcelles* above the chapel of the south tower. The *baptismal font* in the chapel was made by Hans Krumper in 1620. In the middle of the southern aisle is the *Johannes-Altar* by Ignaz Günther (1756). The figures of the Apostles on the pillars in the nave are the work of Faistenberger (St. Andrew), Greiff (St. Paul) and Joseph Prötzner, who also constructed the *pulpit.*

Further on in the direction of Sendlinger Straße, the street Rindermarkt widens

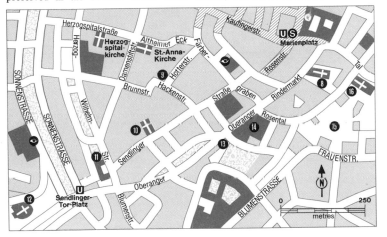

Asamkirche St. Johann Nepomuk

into a square, whose centre forms the *Rinderbrunnen* (cattle fountain), designed by Joseph Henselmann.

Altes Hackenviertel [9]

To get to this old quarter of the city we now turn into *Färbergraben* and reach by way of *Altheimer Eck* the *Herzogspitalstraße* with old Munich buildings: *Weinhaus Neuner*, Nr. 8, *Former Gregorian Seminar*, Nr. 12, which was built by Albrecht V in 1574 to serve as a student dormitory; the present Empire façade dates from the year 1808. In the *Herzogspitalkirche St. Elisabeth*, Nr. 9, the wooden sculpture of the Sorrowing Mary by T. Pader (1651) is of interest. We now go along Damenstiftstraße.

The *St.-Anna-Kirche* (Damenstiftstraße 1) was built by the brothers Gunezrhainer and Asam (stucco and frescoes) in 1733 under Elector Karl Albrecht. The Salesienserinnenkirche (church of Salesians; destroyed in the war) was rebuilt by Erwin Schleich in 1980. Of the endowment for ladies connected to the church, turned into a building in early neo-classical style by Matthias Wissmann in 1785, only the 19-axle façade survived the war.

Turning left in *Brunnstraße* we run into *Hackenstraße*, where the *Radspielerhaus* (Nr. 7) with its neo-classical façade (Jean-Baptiste Metivier, 1817) is worth seeing. The poet Heinrich Heine dwelt here in 1827—1828. Just opposite (Hak-

kenstraße 10) the sculptor Johann Baptist Straub lived, for whom the *rococo house* was erected in 1741. The relief above the portal (six dogs are playing with a ball) has given the house the name of Hundskugel (dog's ball). "Zur Hundskugel" is also the name of Munich's oldest restaurant (1440), located on the corner of Hotterstraße.

Continuing our way down Hackenstraße and turning right into Sendlinger Straße, we cannot fail to notice a corner building on the left side. It is the *Altes Hackerhaus*.

Amidst the shops in *Sendlinger Straße* rises on the right side (Nr. 62) the

*St.-Johann-Nepomuk-Kirche [10]

The church is better known as the *Asam-Kirche*, since Egid Qurin Asam (1692–1750) wanted to build his own private church here. Although Asam had taken over all the costs for the construction of the building, he was forced to make his church accessible to the public after fierce resistance on the part of the citizens. In 1733 the foundation stone was laid, the consecration took place in 1746. The church is one of the most splendid achievements of Bavarian baroque.

The ornate façade tells about the deeds of St. Nepomuk; his life is encompassed in the wooden carvings of the entrance door. The two angels of the gallery's *Bruderschaftsaltar* (fraternity altar) are by Ignaz Günther (1767). They were bought later. The *Gnadenstuhl-Gruppe* (Chair of Mercy Group) with God the Father enthroned and the crucified Christ completes the high altar. In a niche left of the high altar, there is a *statue of Mary* designed by Egid Quirin Asam.

The Asam-Kirche is enframed by the *Priest's House* (1771) on the right and the *Asamhaus* on the left, which was bought by Egid Quirin Asam in 1733.

At the end of Sendlinger Straße is the

Sendlinger Tor [11]

This gateway was erected in 1318, when Ludwig the Bavarian expanded the city and had a second ring of walls built. Of the original fortification only the two sextagonal flanking towers remain.

Across *Sendlinger-Tor-Platz* we can see the Protestant *Matthäuskirche* [12], designed in 1953—1955 by Gustav Gsaenger.

Our way leads back to *Oberanger*, a street parallel to Sendlinger Straße, where we come to (house Nr. 11) the

Ignaz-Günther-Haus [13]

which the famous rococo sculptor acquired in 1761 as a dwelling and workshop. This edifice of Gothic origin was restored in 1977. On the ground floor there is an exhibition about the life and work of the artist.

Between *St.-Jakobs-Platz* (the name-giving church of the square is on the south side), *Oberanger* and *Rosental* we find the

Stadtmuseum [14]

The municipal museum was built in Gothic style towards the end of the 15th century. It originally served as city arsenal. Only the vaulted hall on the ground floor survived the war. Restoration was completed in 1977–1978.

Today the municipal museum houses on the ground floor the *Moriskenraum*, a room with the figures of the *Moriskentänzer* (Moresque dancers) by Erasmus Grasser (1480) and also the *brewery museum* and the *hall of armour*. On the 1st floor special exhibitions relating to the history of the city are on display. The

Viktualienmarkt with St. Peter's

photography museum is lodged here as well. On the 2nd floor are *old Munich rooms* with original furniture from the times between 1700 and 1900. A vast *puppet theatre collection* (examples from all continents and almost all periods) is located on the 3rd floor. The *musical*

instrument collection (all continents, from ancient to modern times) is kept on the 4th floor.

Passing through *Rosental* in an easterly direction, we come to the

2

*Viktualienmarkt [15]

This market is considered the popular centre of the city (see p. 13).

(see p. 13)

Munich's six most popular folk-singers and -comedians have statues commemorating them at this market. The fountain figures represent *Karl Valentin* (1882–1948; designed by Andreas Rauch) and his partner *Liesl Karlstadt* (1892–1960; by Hans Osel), the comedian *Weiß Ferdl* (1883–1949; by Josef Erber), the couplet singer *Roider Jackl* (1906–1975; by Hans Osel), *Elise Aulinger* (1881–1965; by Toni Ruckel) and *Ida Schumacher* (1895–1956; by Marlene Neubauer-Wörner).

Heiliggeistkirche [16]

looks down upon the Viktualienmarkt from the north. The Church of the Holy Ghost is one of the oldest churches in Munich. In the early 13th century Duke Ludwig I had a hospital and a chapel built on this site. In 1327 the great fire completely destroyed both. In 1392 the Gothic hall-church and connecting hospital were finished. In the years 1724–1730 the church's interior was converted totally to baroque style by Johann Georg Ettenhofer and the brothers Asam.

The *high altar* (1727) by Nikolaus Stuber was destroyed, but has been restored. It has a painting by Ulrich Loth (1644); the *angel figures* (about 1730) are originals by Johann Georg Greiff. On the right side of the high altar stands the *Johann-Baptist-Altar* by Antonio Matteo (1730), the painting "The Baptism of Christ" is the work of Melchior Steidl (1720). The church's main treasure, the *Hammerthaler Madonna* (1450), was saved from destruction in the war and now stands in the Marienaltar (Lady altar) in the middle of the north wall. Exactly opposite in the *Kreuzkapelle* (Chapel of the Cross), constructed in 1907, a late-Gothic *cross* (1501) on the south wall is of special interest. Beneath the west gallery the *brass tomb of Duke Ferdinand of Bavaria*, designed by Hans Krumper in 1588, can be seen. The vault frescoes of the brothers Asam were destroyed in the war, but were completely restored by Karl Maninger.

This walk leads through medieval Munich. Its narrow little lanes still retain a strongly medieval character. The tour through the "old town" takes – without a visit to the Deutsches Museum – about one hour and is a continuation of the 2nd walk.

From *Marienplatz* (or the *Heiliggeist-kirche*) turning immediately in front of the main façade of the Old Town Hall, we come to

Burgstraße

This street runs along the northeastern edge of what was formerly the oldest town wall. The slight sloping down to where the moat used to be (a branch of the Isar), can still be seen.

House Nr. 5 was formerly (as of 1550) the *City Scriveners' Office*. It is the only fully preserved late Gothic building in Munich and with its vaulted rooms, leaf-covered yard, and turrets with staircase, as well as its façade, presents a prime example of secular architecture from this period. Today the building houses the "Wein-stadl", a very popular restaurant worth visiting.

In the adjacent *house Nr. 6* (which has been rebuilt in the meantime) the composer Wolfgang Amadeus Mozart had a temporary abode while composing the opera "Idomeneo", which premiered in Munich in 1781.

In *house Nr. 11* the court architect François Cuvilliés died, designer of the Amalienburg and the Alte Residenz. In Burgstraße *Nr. 12* lived and died Wiguläus Freiherr von Kreittmayr (1705–1790), who was an important Bavarian legislator.

A short detour through the *Ledererbogen* (or arch) will lead you to the

Zerwirkgewölbe

an elegant Renaissance building, where even today game and poultry are prepared and sold. In 1591 the first Hof-bräuhaus was built here. In medieval times Ludwig the Stern (1264) had his ducal falconry here.

Burgstraße leads to the archway of the old ducal palace, the

Alter Hof [17]

Ludwig the Stern (1253–1294), having chosen Munich as his place of residence after the first partition of Bavaria, in 1255 had the castle built in the then northeastern part of the city. *Ludwig the Bavarian* (1294–1347), elected German emperor in 1328, made the Munich ducal palace

Palace "Alter Hof"

his imperial residence and kept the imperial insignia in the St. Lorenz Chapel (no longer in existence), which formed the northern part of the Alter Hof. The late Gothic west wing, which was altered under Duke Sigismund in 1460 has been preserved, in spite of later rebuildings and severe damage to the whole complex in the Second World War. Since the restoration work in 1968 the Alter Hof has again acquired most of its medieval form. Even a reconstruction of the façade painting on the little alcove turret decorating the south wing has been attempted in the same way Duke Sigismund had commissioned Gabriel Mäless-kircher to do it.

The Wittelsbachs – with the exception of Sigismund, who continued to use the Alter Hof as his residence when in Munich – saw themselves compelled by civil upheaval to order the construction of a new residence, the so-called new castle on the edge of the city expanded by Ludwig the Bavarian. In consequence of this the Alter Hof became a mainly administrative building. Since 1816 it has housed fiscal offices of the city.

Probably in order to have a connection between the Alter Hof and the new residence, in 1563 Duke Albrecht V (1550–1579) commissioned his court architect Wilhelm Egkl to erect the stables. Since the 19th century the building has served as

Bayerisches Hauptmünzamt [18]

On the ground floor of the later mint were the stables, on the upper stories the ducal art collection as well as the library. The former stable building is of special interest because of its inner courtyard, the *Münzhof* (Mint Yard), 35 by 12 m, divided into three stories, each with glorious leaf-formed arcades. This courtyard is a superb example of Bavarian Renaissance style (at present it is not open to the public). In the 19th century the mint was given new façades. The wall facing the town moat was done in early neo-classical style by Andreas Gärtner and Franz Thurn in 1809. The façade facing Maximilianstraße was designed in 1859–1863 by Friedrich Bürklein. It was meant to fit in with the general architectural concept of the street.

Passing from the Hauptmünzamt through Hofgraben to *Maximilianstraße,* we turn left and after a few steps reach

Post Office Nr. 1 [19]

This palace used to belong to the counts of Törring-Jettenbach, who commissioned the brothers Gunezrhainer to build it in 1747–1754. As early as 1834 Leo von Klenze transformed this building into the main post office. In 1836 Klenze designed the *Loggia* on the north side to provide an appropriate finishing touch for the ducal Max-Joseph-Platz with the Residence and the National Theatre. The frescoes in the Loggia, resembling those of Pompeii, are called "the horse tamers" and are the work of Johann Georg Hiltensperger. The building, damaged during the war, was rebuilt in the years 1952–1953. The *main portal,* which survived the war, has been put in the counter hall. Some of Johann Baptist Straub's figures (1772) have been placed in the vestibule and some in the Bavarian National Museum. They used to adorn the staircase hall.

Walking back to Hofgraben we go through *Pfisterbogen* (or arch) and *Pfisterstraße* and reach a famed tourist attraction, much praised in song, the

*Hofbräuhaus [20]

Originally the ducal, then the royal, and since 1852 the state brewery, it has been in existence since 1589. The present building was designed by Max Littmann and G. Maxon in 1896–1897, whose concept was influenced by old Munich burgher houses. The *tap room* on the ground floor has a cheerful atmosphere, with music and plenty of beer. Nearly every tourist will want to have seen this. In the upper stories, however, the Hofbräuhaus is more refined. In the *festival hall* a brass band plays every evening during the season. On a warm summer evening it is quite pleasant to sit in the *inner courtyard* with its arcades.

Opposite the Hofbräuhaus is the *Platzl,* an old Munich place of amusement with a daily Bavarian folklore programme. In the souvenir shops around here, however, you will hardly find genuine Munich items.

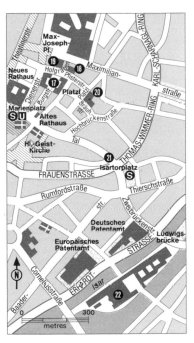

Continuing through *Bräuhausstraße* in an easterly direction and turning right into *Hochbrückenstraße*, we see on the opposite side (house Nr. 8) the *Moradelli-Haus*, a typically old Munich burgher house from the 17th century with a gorgeous courtyard with leaves and balconies around it. It was restored by Erwin Schleich in 1969.

Going on through Hochbrückenstraße we reach the *Tal*. About 200 m to the east is the

Isartor [21]

This gate was part of the fortifications built by Ludwig the Bavarian after he had expanded the city towards the Isar. In 1337 the fortification works for the "outer city" were finished. In 1833 Friedrich von Gärtner was entrusted with the restoration of the gate, in the course of which Bernhard Neher painted a *fresco* on the outside of the main tower in 1835; this work depicts the entry into Munich of Emperor Ludwig the Bavarian after the victorious battle against the Habsburgs at Mühldorf (1322). Polish specialists were hired for the restoration of the Isartor in 1972.

The Isartor houses the *Valentin-Musäum* (see p. 12), a typically Munich-like collection of curiosities, dedicated to the popular comedian Karl Valentin.

The walk continues east towards the Isar to the site where Henry the Lion had the first wooden bridge built, which led to the development of Munich. The present *Ludwigsbrücke* was built in 1934/35. Across the bridge on the right you see the huge complex of the *Deutsches Museum*. Anyone planning to spend a whole extra day in the museum (which is almost necessary, considering the number of objects and exhibits on display) can return to the city centre from Isartor by S-train or tram.

***Deutsches Museum [22]

In 1903 *Oskar von Miller* (1855–1934) had founded the "German Association – Museum for Masterpieces of Natural Science and Technology". As a result of Miller's initiative this technical museum came into existence and – in the course of years – became the largest of its kind in the world. The foundation stone of the main building was laid in 1904 in the presence of Emperor Wilhelm II. Gabriel von Seidl had won the first prize for the plans in a contest. After the death of

Gabriel von Seidl (1914), his brother Emanuel continued the construction. The opening of the museum took place in 1925. From 1928 to 1935 additional buildings (library and congress hall) were designed by German Bestelmeier. During the Second World War 80% of the museum were severely damaged. 20% of the exhibits were destroyed. In its present reconstructed state the museum comprises an exhibition area of 40,000 square metres.

The museum possesses a *library* of 687,000 volumes and 60,000 technical drawings.

Open daily 9 a.m. – 5 p.m., library 9 a.m. – 5 p.m., except for New Year's Day, Good Friday, Easter Sunday, May 1st, Whit Sunday, Corpus Christi, June 17th, All Saints' Day, Christmas Day, December 31st. Admission charge. Tel. 2 17 91.

The tour of the museum is about 16 km long and includes 15,000 items on display. Because of this abundance the visitor is advised to limit his tour according to his particular interests. The following is a list of the various departments. The numbers refer to the numbers of the plans.

Ground floor and basement

1: Mineral resources (with illustrative material on the history of the earth and the evolution of life).

2: Drilling and shaft-sinking (mining).

2a: Mineral gas, mineral oil.

3: Mining (ore mines, mining techniques, salt-mines, coal mines).

4: Mineral dressing (the extraction of raw materials; coking and briquetting).

5: Metallurgy (extraction of non-ferrous metals; the treatment of iron; the production of steel).

6: The treatment of metals (forging, rolling and drawing; moulding and casting; metallic raw materials; welding, flame-cutting and soldering; historical and modern machine tools).

7: Engines (muscle-power machines, wind-power engines, hydrolic power engines; steam engines; water turbines; hot-air engines; internal-combustion engines); closed at present.

8: Land transport (walking aids, sledges and carriages; motor-cars; bicycles and motor bicycles; railways).

9: Motor-cars.

10. Model railway.

11: Open air collection (airplanes, cranes, turbines, windmill).
12: Tunnelling, construction of underground railways.
13: Roads and bridges.
14: Hydraulic engineering.
15: Heavy current engineering (Faraday Cage, generators).
16: Marine navigation (evolution of the ship, development of nautical instruments, underground); closed at present.

1st floor

17: Aeronautics (from balloon and airship to jet propulsion and rocket).
18: Historic instruments.
19: Physics (mechanics of solids, mechanics of liquids and gases; oscillations and waves; heat; electricity, optics).
20: Nuclear physics and technology (including *Otto Hahn's apparatus for nuclear fission).
21: Telecommunications.
22: Musical instruments (valuable historical collection).
23: Chemistry.

2nd floor

24: Prehistoric technology.
25: Glass technology (production and techniques).
26: Industrial chemistry.
27: Technology of paper production.
28: Writing and printing.
29: Photography.
30: Textile technology.

3rd floor

31: Weights and measures.
32: Time measurement (from sun dial to modern quartz technique).
33: Agriculture (arable farming, dairy, sugar manufacture, brewery).
34: Space travel.

5th and 6th floor

Astronomy (history and nature of astronomy) and Planetarium.

Several times a day there are demonstrations in the Planetarium. Movements of heavenly bodies are simulated.

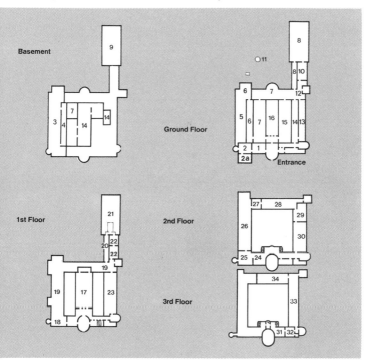

33

This way leads through royal Munich and concentrates on the Residence. If you want to include its museums and theatres, you will need a whole day to see it.

Walking down *Dienerstraße* from *Marienplatz* within five minutes we reach

*Max-Joseph-Platz [23]

The present form of this cobblestone square goes back to Ludwig I (ruled 1825–1848). In the centre of the square is the *bronze statue of Maximilian I Joseph*, erected in his honour by his son Ludwig I. The monument was designed by the Berlin sculptor Christian Daniel Rauch in 1832 and cast by J. B. Stiglmaier. It was unveiled in 1835.

Behind the monument rises the neo-classical façade of the

*Nationaltheater [24]

or National Theatre. Up to the year 1803 there was a Franciscan monastery on this site, which was, however, pulled down in the course of secularization. Since the citizens of Munich had been demanding

National Theatre

an opera house for some time (the Altes Residenztheater was reserved for the royal court) Maximilian I Joseph announced an architectural contest among the great architects of his time. To everyone's surprise this royal competition was won by a 21-year-old newcomer

named *Carl von Fischer*. In 1811 construction was started according to his design of 1802, which had been reworked in some aspects. Crown Prince Ludwig laid the foundation stone of the building. In 1823 the building – completely finished in 1818 – burnt down. 1825 saw the reopening of the opera house, rebuilt by Leo von Klenze according to the original plans. In 1943 the theatre was almost completely destroyed by bombs. Its reconstruction in 1963, true to the original plans, even down to the decoration of the rooms, cost 63 million marks.

Only in the lower pediment were the original plans disregarded. The sculptor Georg Brenninger was commissioned to create a monumental group "Apollo and the Muses", which was placed there in 1972.

To the left of the National Theatre is the modern *Residenztheater* or Residence Theatre [25], which was built between 1948 and 1951 by Karl Hocheder in place of the Altes Residenztheater.

The south side of Max-Joseph-Platz is taken up by *Post Office Nr. 1* (see page 31), the loggia of which was designed by Klenze. The west side is adorned by some *burgher houses in Munich style*, one of which, *Residenzstraße 13* [26] (Eilles-Kaffee), deserves special mention. It has the only Gothic courtyard still existing in Munich, built about 1500 and renovated in 1971. The three-storey *arcaded courtyard* is structured with colonnades and pierced brick-work balustrades.

The northern end of the square is formed by the *Royal Palace of the Residence* (see p. 36).

Here is the entrance to the museum of the Residence and the treasury. The main entrance to the Residence is located in the narrow Residenzstraße.

*RESIDENZ [27]

Because of the rapid growth of the city as well as popular uprisings, the Wittelsbachs in 1385 felt forced to give up their residence, the Alter Hof, and to lay down a "new castle" at the northeast corner of the expanded city. Almost all of the Wittelsbachs contributed to the building or had older edifices torn down to make room for new projects. The only survival over the centuries is the so-called Moritz Tower. As a result of the various plans and styles, the Munich Residence is certainly not a perfect architectural unity, but it is a most interesting exhibition of cultural history.

The **Maximlianische Residenz** or Maximilian Residence [a] extends along Residenzstraße. It was erected between 1611 and 1619 by Hans Krumper and Heinrich Schön. After the Second World War it got back its original Renaissance façade with 35 axes, which is accentuated by two marble portals. The painting was by Hermann Kaspar. In a raised niche between the portals stands the *Patrona Boiariae,* a bronze statue of the Virgin created by Hans Krumper in 1616. This figure, which was commissioned by Elector Maximilian I, actually became the Bavarian patron saint. Krumper also designed the *Allegories of the Four Cardinal Virtues,* which decorate the slanting gables of the marble portals. The *escutcheon holding lions,* two in front of each entrance, are the work of Hubert Gerhard.

The left portal leads to the *Kaiserhof* or Emperor's Court [b], the façade of which was created anew by Hermann Kaspar.

This quadratic open space joins the *Apothekenhof* or Chemist's Shop Court [c] to the east, which Maximilian I had already built. It was restored, however, in the form it was given later on by Ludwig I. From 1832 to 1842 Leo von Klenze worked on the *festive hall* (see p. 38) to the left, which has a terrace and an outside staircase towards the Apothekenhof. To the east, in the so-called *Apothekenflügel* or wing [d], are the rooms of the Academy of Sciences. On the south (to the right hand) is the

*Brunnenhof or Fountain's Court [e], the earliest edifice of which, the **Antiquarium* [f] (see p. 36) takes up the right length side; Albrecht V (1550–1579) gave order for its construction. Maximilian I commissioned Hans Krumper to complete this courtyard in the form of a longstretched octagon (1610–1620, restored in 1958). The *Wittelsbach fountain* stands dominant in the middle of the square. Hubert Gerhard designed the bronze figures between 1611 and 1614. At the feet of Duke Theodor (about 700) are four mermen symbolizing the four most important Bavarian rivers. The fountain is embellished with gods, animals and putti.

From the Brunnenhof we enter the

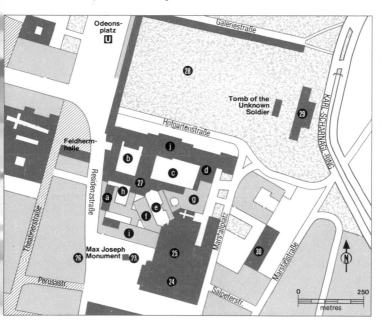

Altes Residenztheater or Old Residence Theatre [g], which is world famous under the name of its designer as the *Cuvilliéstheater*. This masterpiece of rococo style was originally located where the present Residenztheater stands. Elector Maximilian III Joseph had it constructed outside the Residence in 1751 as a fire precaution, after a fire in the Georgssaal, which had served before as a theatre room in the "new castle". The Cuvilliéstheater found its present location after the war, when the destroyed Brunnenhof layout was reconstructed. Because the ****inner decorations had been brought in safety during the war, the original majesty of this rococo jewel created by François Cuvilliés (1731–1777) can be admired again. *(Open Mon.–Sat. 2–5 p.m., Sun. 10 a.m. – 5 p.m., admission charge).*

We leave the Brunnenhof to the western corner and enter the *Kapellenhof* or Chapel's Court [h], where we pass the entrance of the *Staatliche Münzsammlung* or State Coin Collection. The Kapellenhof leads back to Residenzstraße, which runs into Max-Joseph-Platz on the left. The

*Königsbau or Royal Palace [i], bordering the square on the north side, was built between 1826 and 1835 at the command of Ludwig I. The architect was Leo von Klenze, who, applying designs of Carl von Fischer, expanded the façade to include 21 bays. The three-storey middle

section was patterned on the Palazzo Pitti in Florence. The façade is of sandstone with diamond-patterned rustication. The Königsbau was used for the apartments of Ludwig I. The middle portal is the entrance to the Residenzmuseum and the treasury (see page 12).

*Residenzmuseum

On the right side of the hall is the entrance to the **Schatzkammer* or treasury (see p. 12) with crowns and gems, goldsmiths' work and jewels from 10 centuries. It is located in rooms I–X and must be visited separately.

The numbers given in the following survey are according to the official numbering of the rooms in the Residence Museum. A viewing of rooms 1–81 is recommended for a morning tour; rooms 82–112 can then be seen in the afternoon.

1: Vestibule to the Königsbau court (ground floor façade by Cuvilliés the Elder)

2 and 3: Garden Halls (sculptures, including **Bavaria* by Hubert Gerhard)

4: **Ancestors' Gallery* (erected by Joseph Effner from 1726–1731; 121 portraits of Wittelsbach rulers)

5: **Porcelain Cabinet* (also by Effner)

6: **Grotto Court* (designed by Friedrich Sustris for Wilhelm V about 1580; the **Perseus Fountain* is the work of Hubert Gerhard)

7: **Antiquarium* or Hall of Antiquities

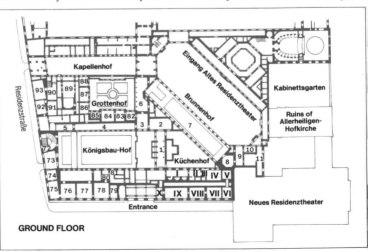

GROUND FLOOR

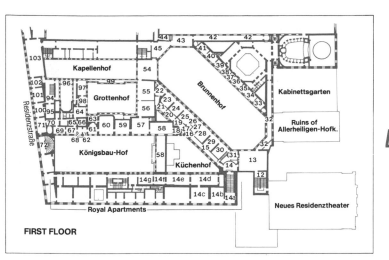

FIRST FLOOR

(This important Renaissance room was built for Albrecht V by Wilhelm Egkl and Jacobo Strada from 1569–1571. It was remodelled in 1586–1600 by Friedrich Sustris. Built to house the duke's collection of antiquities, it was later used as a festive hall.)

8: Octagon

9: Doorway (nice view of the Brunnenhof)

10: Room with Hercules relief

11 and 12: Passage and staircase to the Black Hall

13: Black Hall (so named due to the former dark paintings by Hans Werle and Christoph Schwarz)

14: Yellow Staircase (leading to the royal apartments of Ludwig I and Therese)

14 a–g: Halls of Battles (originally rooms for Ludwig I, now decorated with battle scenes). Porcelain rooms (with fine porcelain of French manufactures as well as of Nymphenburg and Berlin)

15: Elector's rear apartments (porcelain collection, mainly from East Asia)

22–31: *Elector's rooms* (decorated with restrained luxury between 1746 and 1763 by François Cuvilliés the Elder)
Alle Saints' Passage (frescoes by Carl Rottmann, about 1830)

33–41: Former Hofgarten rooms (designed in 1612 by Charles Pierre Puille and expanded to house Princess Charlotte in 1814, for this reason now called "Charlottentrakt")

42: Charlottengang (earlier passageway to the "Neufeste", with stucco from 1613)

43 and 44: Vestibule and Broad Staircase (about 1600)

45: Vestibule to St. George Hall of Knights

46–53: Kaiserhoftraktzimmer or rooms (with Trier passage way dating from 1612, Knights' room, Hall for Audience, Conference Room; ceiling frescoes by Peter Candid)

54: St. George Hall of Knights

55–62: **Reiche Zimmer* or Rich Apartments (The original rooms, designed by Joseph Effner for Elector Karl Albrecht in 1726, were burnt out in 1729. François Cuvilliés converted these rooms into masterpieces of rococo, with the aid of Johann Baptist Zimmermann, who did the painting.)

63: Chinese Cabinet

64 and 65: Cloakroom and passage way to

66–71: *Papal Rooms* (so named because Pope Pius VI lived in these rooms in 1782. These elegant baroque rooms were designed by Agostino Barelli in 1665–1667; there are some well-preserved paintings by Stefano Catani here)

72: Queen Mother's Staircase

73: Passage to Königsbauhof

74: Anteroom to

75–79: the Halls of the Nibelungs (designed by Leo von Klenze in 1827–1834 for Ludwig I; the paintings illustrat-

37

ing the Nibelung saga are by Julius Schnorr von Carolsfeld)

80 and 81: Passage way and staircase to the Königsbau.

On the afternoon tour we go through rooms 1–3 to

82–88: Yellow Rooms (designed by François Cuvilliés the Elder about 1730, today containing a collection of 18th-century European porcelaine)

89: Court chapel (built 1601–1603)

90: Lower landing of chapel staircase

91–93: Vestment rooms (fine collection of ecclesiastical vestments)

94: Chapel staircase

95: Reliquary cabinet (valuable ecclesiastical objects)

96: Gallery of the court chapel

97 and 98: Vestibule and Reiche Kapelle or Rich Chapel (private chapel of Maximilian I, designed by Hans Krumper in 1607)

99: Passage with antlers (etchings by Ridinger)

100–103: Former cabinet meeting rooms and Hartschiersaal (now used as a silver room with objects from the 17th and 18th century)

104–111: Stone rooms (constructed between 1612 and 1617, general design by Hans Krumper. Maximilian I had all these rooms painted; some of the work was by Peter Candid and Johann Anton Gumpp. Room 111 contains Duke Albrecht V's fayence collection)

112: Theatiner passageway.

The *north section* [j] of the Residence, the façade of which (today restored) was constructed by Leo von Klenze for Ludwig I, contains the *Kaisertreppe* or Emperor's staircase (1616). This impressive structure from the late Renaissance is situated at the entrance to the *Staatliche Sammlung Ägyptischer Kunst* or State Collection of Egyptian Art (see p. 12). The

Festsaalbau or Festive Hall predominates the north section, which today contains the *Herkulessaal* (concert hall), with architecture strongly influenced by Palladio. The 250 m-long building was erected according to designs by Klenze. The figures were made by Ludwig Schwanthaler, who also created the bronze statues decorating the ground floor.

Opposite the north section is the

Hofgarten with Theatinerkirche

*Hofgarten [28] or court gardens, which was laid out at the time of Maximilian I. In the middle of this park in the French style there is a *circular temple,* probably the work of Heinrich Schön (1615). Its roof is crowned by a copy of the Bavaria modelled by Herbert Gerhard in 1594. The putti are copies of lost works by Hans Krumper.

The *Hofgarten arcades,* including the gateway designed by Klenze, were restored in 1950. The frescoes in the arcades on either side of the gateway were by Wilhelm von Kaulbach (restored). In the northern wing of the arcades are the rooms of the Kunstverein (society of arts), private galleries, and the *Theatermuseum* or Theatre Museum (see p. 12). Richard Seewald painted the pictures on the walls in 1961.

The *Tomb of the Unknown Soldier* at the east end of the Hofgarten was constructed by Bernhard Bleeker in 1924.

Behind the tomb towers the copula of the former *Armeemuseum* or Army Museum [29]. The ruin of this edifice, constructed by Ludwig Mellinger from 1900 to 1905, is to be rebuilt.

To the south we come to *Marstallplatz,* on the left side of which is the

Former Hofreitschule [30] or Court Riding School and the *Marstall* or stables, built between 1817 and 1822 by Leo von Klenze. This neo-classical building contains scenery for the State Theatre and is used for the experimental stage of the "Theater im Marstall".

Further south comes *Maximilianstraße;* by turning right we soon return to *Max-Joseph-Platz,* our starting point.

This walk takes us through an extension of the city planned by Maximilian I Joseph, but mainly carried through by the involvement of Crown Prince Ludwig. This part of town is called *Maxvorstadt* and was built between 1816 and 1852. The tour, beginning at Odeonsplatz (underground-station), lasts approximately two hours.

*Odeonsplatz

Ludwig I commissioned the layout of the square and the Ludwigstraße, which begins here. While still crown prince he entrusted the design to Leo von Klenze, who had just arrived in Munich. In 1827, two years after taking the throne, Ludwig chose Friedrich von Gärtner to supervise the construction. So the

Feldherrnhalle [31]

or Generals' Hall was the work of Gärtner (erected 1841–1844) and not of Klenze, who was responsible for the rest of the neo-classical buildings from Odeonsplatz to Theresienstraße. The model for this hall was the Loggia dei Lanzi in Florence. In the left adjoining arch stands the bronze figure of *Count Tilly,* the Bavarian commander during the Thirty Years' War; his counterpart on the other side is the statue of *Prince Wrede,* who fought against the French in 1814. Both of these standing figures were cast by Ferdinand von Miller, according to sketches by Ludwig Schwanthaler. The *memorial commemorating the victory of the Bavarian army* in the war of 1870/1871 on the rear wall is also the work of Miller.

The Feldherrnhalle backs on to the

Preysing-Palais [32]

in Residenzstraße. Joseph Effner was commissioned to build this rococo palace by Count Maximilian von Preysing in 1723–1728. The walls on the outside, which are carefully structured and are accented by elaborately decorated portals, are embellished with stucco in the rococo style. Going through Preysing-Passage to Theatinerstraße, we encounter one of the most prominent edifices at Odeonsplatz, the

*Theatinerkirche [33]

The founding of Theatiner Church is related to a religious oath sworn by Henriette Adelaide of Savoy, the wife of Elector Ferdinand Maria, in 1659. In gratitude for the birth of a male-heir prince, she wanted to have a court church built, which would also serve as monastery church for the Theatiner monks.

After the birth of Crown Prince Max Emanuel (1662), Ferdinand Maria commissioned the Italian architect Agostino Barelli to design a church which would put everything else in the shade. Barelli used the Roman church St. Andrea della Valle as his model. The St. Kajetan Church introduced the baroque style in Munich and was in turn used as model for later edifices built by Bavarian electors.

After Barelli had fallen into disfavour in 1667, Enrico Zuccalli took over the artistic direction of the project. He came from a family of masons, who had immigrated to Bavaria from the Grisons in Switzerland. Zuccalli decided the shape of the dome and the towers. The ultimate design for the façade remained undecided for a long time. For this reason, although the Theatinerkirche was consecrated in 1675, it received its final form at the hands of François Cuvilliés almost a century later in 1768.

While the towers and dome fully comply with the baroque plan envisaged by Zuccalli, the façade by Cuvilliés almost in Empire style contrasts with the baroque splendor of the church. The four *figures of founders* (St. Maximilian, St. Kajetan, St. Ferdinand, and St. Adelheid) are the work of Roman Anton Boos.

The interior (a central aisle with five bays, with side chapels, transept, and choir), divided into three parts, has its walls and ceiling elaborately decorated with stucco: the Italian influence is clearly to be seen. Wolfgang Leutner created the stucco figures in full relief, while Nicolo Petri was responsible for the stucco decorations (1685–1688). The *high altar* is a copy of the original, which was destroyed. Caspar de Crayer painted the picture "Mary on the Throne" in 1646. At the west wall of the northern transept is the entrance to the *royal vault,* in which Ferdinand Maria, Max

5

39

Emanuel, Karl Albrecht, Maximilian III Joseph, Karl Theodor, King Max I, King Otto of Greece and Crown Prince Ruprecht are buried.

In the northern part of the transept stands the *Altar of Mary* with the painting "The Holy Familiy" by Carlo Cignani (1676). The "Annunciation to Mary" is by George Demareés, the St. Mark

In Schwabing

statue by Balthasar Ableithner (1672). In the southern part of the transept there is the *St. Kajetan Altar* with the painting "The Intercession of St. Kajetan", created by Joachim Sandrart in 1671. Balthasar Ableithner was responsible for the statue of St. John. The great black pulpit is a work of Andreas Faistenberger (1686). The Descent from the Cross painting in the middle southern side chapel was made by a pupil of Tintoretto.

North of the Theatinerkirche is the *Moy-Palais*. This was the first neo-classical edifice built in Ludwigstraße and was a work of Leo von Klenze (1819).

Odeon [34]

In 1826—1828 Ludwig I commissioned Leo von Klenze with the construction of an Academy of Music. Today the building houses the *Bavarian Ministry of the Interior.* Ludwig instructed Klenze to adapt the façade to that of the

Leuchtenberg-Palais [35]

which Klenze had built in 1816—1821 for Eugène de Beauharnais, the stepson of Napoleon and the son-in-law of Maximilian I Joseph. The former Viceroy of Italy was living in exile in Munich with the title

Duke of Leuchtenberg. Klenze supposedly used the Palazzo Farnese in Rome as his model. Today the building serves as the *Bavarian Ministry of Finance.*

Opposite these last two buildings mentioned is the *Basargebäude* [36], a neoclassical building that Klenze built in 1824—1826 to provide a boundary between Odeonsplatz and Hofgarten.

Reiterdenkmal Ludwigs I. [37]

The equestrian statue of Ludwig I was dedicated to the king by the city of Munich in 1862. The monument was designed by one of Schwanthaler's pupils, Max von Widenmann.

Continuing north from Odeonsplatz and walking along *Ludwigstraße* we see on the right side a building erected during the Third Reich, which interrupts the harmony of the street as designed by Leo von Klenze. It now houses the *Bavarian Ministry for Food, Agriculture, and Forestry.*

Klenze's original pattern, however, was followed in the reconstruction of a *business house at Ludwigstraße 6—12,* which was destroyed in the war. The building contains among other offices the Bank of America and the Academy for Political Science. In 1822—1823 Klenze had linked here together the façades of three dwelling houses in the style of Florentine Renaissance.

The next building on the right side of the street, the

Former Bayerisches Kriegsministerium [38]

or Bavarian War Ministry is the last building Klenze erected in Ludwigstraße (1824—1830). This former ministry, reconstructed in 1966, now houses the *Bavarian State Archives* and the *Institute for Bavarian History.*

From this point Friedrich von Gärtner took over the further development of Ludwigstraße in 1832. After long disputes with Ludwig I, leading three times to a change of plans, Gärtner built from 1832 to 1839 the

Bayerische Staatsbibliothek [39]

or Bavarian State Library with a façade of 155 m and 25 window bays. The building incorporates stylistic elements from the Florentine Palazzo Strozzi. In front of the building there is a flight of steps on either side of the entrance, which is decorated with the statues of Homer, Thucydides, Aristotle, and Hippocrates (going from right to left). The principal sight on the inside of the state library is the staircase with its monolithic pillars and Corinthian capitals.

Opposite the state library there are the buildings of a *former Endowment for Ladies* and a *former Institute for the Blind,* both designed by Gärtner in 1840–1843.

Pfarrkirche St. Ludwig [40]

The first plans for the construction of the parish church of St. Ludwig had already been submitted to the king by Leo von Klenze. The king was, however, far from being enthralled by the idea of a basilica with low aisles. So it was Friedrich von Gärtner's task to erect the church in the years 1829–1844 in the way it has been reconstructed by Erwin Schleich after its destruction in the war. The church is now in the form of a basilica with three aisles. The façade with flanking towers, the cubic *rectory* (on the left) and *Gärtner's former residence* (to the right; now the University Construction Office) form a splendid unity emphasized by arcades, galleries, and the arches of the vestibule. The statues in the façade niches (Christ and the four Evangelists) are by Ludwig Schwanthaler.

The interior of the church, patterned on Romanesque forms, is dominated by

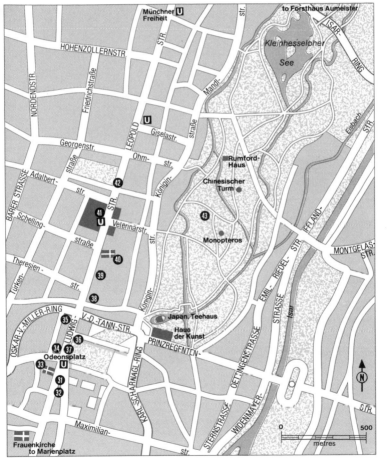

frescoes. The great fresco in the choir *The Last Judgement* is by Peter Cornelius (1836–1840). Covering a surface of 18.3 by 11.3 m, it is, next to Michelangelo's "Last Judgement" in the Sixtine Chapel, one of the largest church frescoes.

At the end of Ludwigstraße King Ludwig I envisaged a counterpart to Odeonsplatz at its beginning, a forum of science. So Gärtner designed a square in 1835–1840, flanked on one side by the *Georgianum* (a seminary for Catholic priests) and on the other side by the

Universität [41]

or university. The triple-winged complex around Geschwister-Scholl-Platz (as it is called today in memory of the leaders of the "White Rose", a resistance group during the Third Reich) was conceived by Gärtner in a neo-classical Romanesque style. The main building of the university with its 27 axes and its three-storied façade is symmetrically laid out. The two fountains patterned by Gärtner like Roman fountains are symmetrically arranged on an axis leading from the main entrance of the university to Veterinärstraße.

South of Veterinärstraße stands the already mentioned *Georgianum*. It was built by Gärtner in 1835–1839. Further north is the former *Max-Joseph-Stift*, an "educational institute for daughters from the upper class", which had been founded by Maximilian I Joseph in 1809. Ludwigstraße ends at the

Siegestor [42]

or Triumphal Arch. In 1844 Gärtner began the construction. After his death in 1847, the monument was finished by Eduard Metzger in 1852. The model for the triple gate was the Arch of Constantine in Rome. King Ludwig I had the Siegestor erected to commemorate the achievements of the Bavarian Army in the Wars of Liberation of 1814–1815.

The gate has attained topical importance through the recently added words of Wilhelm Hausenstein: "Dedicated to victory, destroyed by war, an exhortation to peace." In 1972 the Quadriga (restored by Elmar Dietz), which had fallen down due to damages to the arch, was put back in its original place.

West of the Siegestor is the *Academy of Fine Arts,* built by Gottfried Neureuther in Venetian Renaissance style (1874–1887).

North of the Siegestor begins a town-district known as *Schwabing.* By day – with the exception of the Leopoldstraße – Schwabing is a sober and respectable suburb. At night, however, the streets are filled with artists and would-be artists. the curious and those hungry for pleasure and entertainment.

Returning to the university and then going down *Veterinärstraße* we come to

*Englischer Garten [43]

or English Garden. The park was laid out in the meadows of the Isar under Elector Karl Theodor in 1789 according to plans drawn up by the American *Benjamin Thompson,* better known as *Count Rumford* (1753–1814). The garden was developed from 1804 onwards by the landscape gardener *Ludwig von Sckell.* The English Garden has its name because of its informal "English" style and is one of Europe's largest city parks.

Our way takes us straight into the park from Veterinärstraße. After crossing the so-called Eisbach (ice brook), we see on the left the *Monopteros,* a circular, neo-classical temple in Roman style with Ionic capitals. Ludwig I commissioned Leo von Klenze to build it in 1837–1838 as a memorial to Elector Karl Theodor. The Monopteros provides a marvellous view of the park.

From this circular temple we continue north and soon reach the *Chinese Tower,* which was built in 1790–1791 by Joseph Frey. It burnt down in the Second World War, but was reconstructed in 1952 according to the original plans. In 1790 Johann Baptist Lechner built the *Ökonomiegebäude* (economy building; now used as a restaurant), as well as the nearby *Rumford House.*

From this building a path leads straight north (crossing an asphalt road cutting through the park) to the *Kleinhesseloher See,* an artificial pond laid out in 1799–1812. There are long walks in a northerly direction, e.g. to the *Forsthaus Aumeister* (restaurant; 45 minutes) or to the *Isar meadows.* You can also turn round at the lake and follow a path along the Eisbach leading to the *Haus der Kunst* or House of Art. Just before this building, which marks the end of the English Garden on the downtown side, there is a *Japanese tea-house,* which was built by Mitsuo Nomura in 1972 on the occasion of the 20th Olympic Summer Games as Japan's present to the city of Munich. – You can return by bus to the inner city.

6th Walk. The Buildings of the Nobility: *Odeonsplatz – *Wittelsbacherplatz – Promenadeplatz – Lenbachplatz – Alter Botanischer Garten

This walk leads through the former *Kreuzviertel* and takes about an hour.

From *Odeonsplatz* (underground) we go down *Brienner Straße*, where after 100 m

*Wittelsbacherplatz [44]

opens to the right. In the middle of the square is the *equestrian statue of Elector Maximilian I* (1597–1651). The rider on the pedestal designed by Leo von Klenze is the work of Bertel Thorvaldsen.

On the north side of the square is the *Prinz-Ludwig-Ferdinand-Palais,* built by Xaver Widmann in 1822. The façade design is probably the work of Leo von Klenze, who lived in the palace for 25 years. Prince Ludwig Ferdinand moved into the building in 1878.

A short trip leads from Wittelsbacherplatz along Brienner Straße in a westerly direction to the

Almeida-Palais [45]

The Almeida Palace was erected by Métivier in the years 1823–1824. The elegant neo-classical façade was restored after the war. The adjacent buildings on the right were designed by Leo von Klenze. – Turning back and crossing Brienner Straße we reach *Salvatorplatz* by way of *Amiraplatz*. On the left is the

Bayerisches Kultusministerium [46]

The building of the Bavarian Ministry of Culture and Education formerly was part of the Theatine monastery, which was mostly destroyed in the Second World War. It used to house the monastic library until the secularization of 1803. The

Former Salvatorkirche [47]

gave the square its name. Salvator Church was built as the chapel for the graveyard of the parish "to Our Beloved Lady" by Lukas Rottaler in 1494, who succeeded Jörg von Halspach (builder of the Frauenkirche) as city architect. The late-Gothic brick church, on whose northern façade remnants of old frescoes can be seen, has served as a house of worship for the Greek Orthodox Community since 1829.

Salvatorplatz runs into *Kardinal-Faulhaber-Straße.* House Nr. 7 (left) is the

*Erzbischöfliches Palais [48]

or Archbishop's Palace. In 1733–1737 François Cuvilliés the Elder built this palace together with Johann Baptist Zimmermann for the Count of Holstein, son of Elector Karl Albrecht. The building has been the residence of the archbishops of Munich and Freising since 1818.

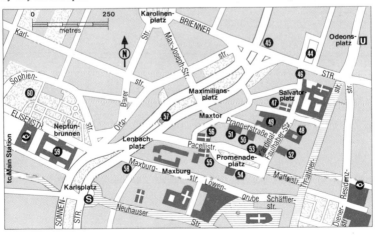

43

Across from the Archbishop's Palace *Prannerstraße* branches off. House Nr. 2 is equally worth looking at, the

Preysing-Palais [49]

This palace is the work of François Cuvilliés the Elder, who designed a rococo façade here. On the other side of the street (house Nr. 7) is the

Palais Seinsheim [50]

This noble palace with its rococo façade was probably built about 1760. Right next to it (house Nr. 9) is the

Palais Gise [51]

It was also probably built about 1760 in rococo style by Cuvilliés' pupil Karl Albert von Lespilliez. Only the façade of this building remains, which was commissioned by Baron von Gise.

We turn back to Kardinal-Faulhaber-Straße and follow it in the direction of Promenadeplatz. On the left side (house Nr. 12) is the

Palais Porcia [52]

It was built by Enrico Zuccalli in 1693–1694 for Count Fugger. In 1731 Elector Karl Albrecht acquired the palace and gave it to his mistress, Countess Morawitzky, later Princess Porcia. For her François Cuvilliés redid the façade in rococo style in 1737.

At the corner of Promenadeplatz (house Nr. 2) is the

Palais Montgelas [53]

Emanuel Joseph von Herigoyen built it for Count Montgelas in 1810/1811. This neo-classical building is today part of the hotel "Bayerischer Hof".

We pass the lawn of the square – statues here commemorate the composer *Orlando di Lasso* (1532–1594), Elector *Max Emanuel* (1679–1726), the composer *Christoph Willibald Gluck* (1714–1787) and the Bavarian historian *Lorenz von Westenrieder* (1748–1829) – and reach the

Gunezrhainerhaus [54]

About 1730 the court architect Johann Baptist Gunezrhainer had this house built for himself.

On the southwest corner of Promenadeplatz stands the

Karmeliterkirche [55]

Karmeliter Church is the earliest baroque church in Munich. Its construction dates back to a vow by Elector Maximilian I (1597–1651). The church was, however, first consecrated under Elector Ferdinand Maria in the year 1660. From 1802 to 1811 Schedel von Greiffenstein created the façade in neo-classical style.

Promenadeplatz turns into *Pacellistraße*. On the right is the

*Dreifaltigkeitskirche [56]

Holy Trinity Church was built in 1711–1718 according to the plans of Giovanni Antonio Viscardi by Johann Georg Ettenhofer and Enrico Zuccalli. The church was the fulfilment of a vow made by the citizens of Munich during the War of the Spanish Succession. In the pediment niche a *bronze figure of St. Michael* (modelled on a design by Josef Fichtl) deserves attention. In the interior of the church *wall-stuccos* by Johann Georg Bader (1715) are worth looking at. The tambourless cupola has a *ceiling painting* by Cosmas Damian Asam (1715).
Across from the church is the rebuilt tower of the former *Herzog-Max-Burg* (Duke Max Castle).

Lenbachplatz is separated from Maximiliansplatz by the

Wittelsbacherbrunnen [57]

This fountain was designed in 1893–1895 by Adolf von Hildebrand. The man slinging a stone and the woman offering a bowl of water, between two animal figures, symbolize the destructive and healing power of water.

At the southeast corner of Lenbachplatz is the *Künstlerhaus* [58], the artists' house. It was built by Gabriel von Seidl in 1893–1900. Directly opposite is the

Justizpalast [59]

The law courts, built by Friedrich von Thiersch, are among the most impressive constructions of the late 19th century. Elements of late Renaissance are mixed with baroque forms.

North of the Justizpalast is the

Alter Botanischer Garten [60]

The Old Botanical Garden was laid out by Ludwig von Sckell in 1808–1814 as part of the so-called Max-Vorstadt or suburb.

7th Walk. Munich and its Museums:
Alter Botanischer Garten – St. Bonifaz – Königsplatz – Karolinenplatz – *Lenbachhaus – ***Alte und **Neue Pinakothek

From *Karlsplatz* or *Lenbachplatz* (S-Bahn and trams) the *Old Botanical Garden* (see p. 44) is in easy reach.

We walk through the park, follow *Meiserstraße,* and turn left at *Karlsstraße.* On the other side of the street is the

St.-Bonifaz-Basilika [61]

Commissioned by Ludwig I, St. Boniface Basilica was built by Friedrich Ziebland in 1835–1847. The architect had before been sent by the king to Italy to study early Christian church architecture. Ziebland erected a basilica with 5 naves and 17 beams in the interior. Ludwig I, who allowed Benedictine monks to move in here, chose the church as a final resting place for himself and his wife Therese.

Returning to *Meiserstraße* and following it to the north, we see on the right side of the street the building of the

*Staatliche Graphische Sammlung [62]

In the State Collection of the Graphic Arts hand drawings and graphic prints from late Gothic up to present times are preserved (see p. 12). Opposite there is the building of the *Hochschule für Musik* [63], the music academy. The edifice was used in the Third Reich as a congress hall. In 1938 the "Munich Agreement" between Hitler, Chamberlain, Daladier, and Mussolini was signed here. Between the two buildings *Brienner Straße* leads to *Karolinenplatz.* In the middle of the square stands the

Obelisk [64]

commissioned by Ludwig I and designed by Leo von Klenze. The 29 m-high monument with its twelve brass plates around a brick core was unveiled in 1833. It is meant to commemorate the 30,000 Bavarian soldiers who perished in Napoleon's Russian campaign in 1812. We return to

Königsplatz

Conceived by Carl von Fischer for Ludwig I, this square was, however, laid out by Leo von Klenze. Here Ludwig I wanted to express in visible form his pre-

dilection for classical Greece. At the north of Königsplatz is the

*Glyptothek [65]

Leo von Klenze, taking up the designs of Carl von Fischer for the construction (1816–1830) erected this edifice. It was meant to harbour the royal collection of antique sculpture, as a four-winged complex grouped around a square inner court. The *neo-classical front* was adorned with Ionic columns by Klenze. Above the portico stands a pediment with figures representing Athena surrounded by artists (Johann Martin von Wagner, 1818). In the niches of the wings are statues of Hephaestus, Prometheus, Daedalus, Phidias, Pericles, and Hadrian.

In the halls of the Glyptothek, which was provided with larger windows facing the courtyard during its reconstruction in 1972 (Josef Wiedemann), Greek and Roman sculpture from ancient times on (6th century B.C.) are on display. Of special interest are the *Greek statues of adolescents* (room 1), the *torso of Apollo by Polycletes* (room 2), *statues by Praxiteles*

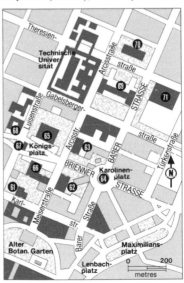

7

45

(room 5) and the **Aeginates,* two groups of sculptures from the tympanums of the temple of Aphaia at Aegina (rooms 7–9). These sculptures, created between 500 and 485 B.C., depict the combats between Greeks and Trojans and were acquired by Crown Prince Ludwig in 1812.

The south of Königsplatz is dominated by the

**Staatliche Antikensammlung [66]

or State Collection of Classical Art. Commissioned by Ludwig I, Georg Friedrich Ziebland designed this "royal art-exhibition building" in 1838–1848 in Corinthian style. The *statues in the pediment* (Bavaria as protectress of arts) were modelled according to plans by Schwanthaler. From 1869 to 1872 this building housed the "Royal Antiquarium". From 1898 to 1912 the "Munich Secession" resided here. From 1919 on the building contained the "New State Gallery". Since its restoration, performed on the outside according to the original plans after the Second World War (1967), this edifice has housed the "Staatliche Antikensammlung" (State Collection of Antiquities), which was put together from *Ludwig I's collection of vases* and from the *Royal Antiquarium.* Among the masterpieces the **Attic vases* are especially worth noticing. Apart from pottery from Crete and Mycenae, terracottas, small bronzes and jewelry are on display. The frescoes in the upper storey are by Carl Rottmann.

Brienner Straße is interrupted at Königsplatz by the

Propyläen [67]

Thus Königsplatz obtained a sort of frame on its western side. Leo von Klenze had been commissioned by Ludwig I to design it. The king approved the design the day after his abdication on March 21st 1848. The Propyläen, taking their name from the west entrance to the Acropolis in Athens, express the close link between Bavaria and Greece. Prince Otto, the second son of Ludwig I, had been crowned king of Greece in 1832. The *sculptures in the pediment* are the work of Ludwig Schwanthaler. These sculptures and the *reliefs on the towers* are witness to the Bavarian-Greek relationship; included in them is the oath of allegiance sworn by the people of Greece to King Otto.

In *Luisenstraße* is the

*Städtische Galerie [68]

The Municipal Gallery is also known as the *Lenbachhaus,* because the painter Franz von Lenbach had this villa built in Florentine Renaissance style by Gabriel von Seidl in 1887. In 1927–1929 the north wing was added by Hans Grässel. Since 1929 the building has been the property of the city, which uses it to house its collection of paintings.

Whereas the north wing is reserved for changing exhibitions, the main building and Lenbach's former studio house contain a collection of paintings from the 19th and 20th centuries, which includes the *Munich School,* Munich landscape painting and Romantic painters (Adam, Dillis, Kobell, Spitzweg) as well as the large *Gabriele-Münter-Collection* with works by Kandinsky and the group of artists called *Der Blaue Reiter.*

Continuing north through Luisenstraße, then turning right on *Gabelsbergerstraße* we pass the *Technical University* (1906–1909, built by German Bestelmeyer). Between *Arcisstraße* and *Barer Straße* in the middle of a park is the

***ALTE PINAKOTHEK [69]

The Old Pinakothek is one of the world's most famous picture galleries. Ludwig I initiated its construction, commissioning Leo von Klenze to work out a plan. The foundation stone was laid in 1826, the museum was opened in 1836.

The best way to tour the museum is by starting on the first floor, where the most famous paintings are to be found. The following list briefly mentions the various rooms and departments:

Early Flemish school (rooms I and IIa): among others Roger van der Weyden "Adoration of the Magi" and "St. Luke painting the Virgin", Hans Memling "The Seven Joys of Mary" and "Mary in the Rose Garden", Lucas van Leyden "Virgin with Donor"

Early German School (rooms II, IIb, and III): among others Dürer "Four Apostles", "Paumgartner-Altar" and "Self-portrait in a fur coat", Matthias Grünewald "St. Erasmus and Mauritius", Lukas Cranach the Elder "The Crucified Christ" and "Battle of Alexander"

Italian School (rooms IV and V): among others Raffael "Madonna Tempi" and "The Holy Family", Fra Filippo Lippi

"The Annunciation to Mary", Botticelli "Lamentation of Christ", Titian "The Crown of Thorns" and "Emperor Karl V", Tintoretto "The Gonzago Cycle", Veronese "Mary with Child and Donor"

Flemish School (rooms VI, VII, and VIII): among others van Dyck "Rest during the Flight", Rubens "Last Judgment", "The Honeysuckle Arbor", "The Rape of the Daughters of Leukippos", "The Drunken Silenus", "The Virgin wearing a Rose Garland", "Hélène Fourment with Son Frans" and "The Massacre of the Children at Bethlehem"

Dutch School (room IX): among others Rembrandt "The Holy Family", "The Sacrificing of Isaac", Hals "Willem van Heythuysen"

Italian Baroque School (room X): among others Tiepolo "Adoration of the Magi", Reni "The Ascension of Mary"

French School (rooms XI, XIIa, and XII): among others Poussin "Lamentation of Christ", Lorrain "The Expulsion of Hagar", Fragonard "Girl with Dog", Boucher "Girl Resting", "Marquise de Pompadour" and "Idyll in the Country"

Venetian School (room XIIb): among others Guardi "Clock-tower at St. Mark's Square"

Spanish School (room VIII): among others El Greco "The Disrobing of Christ", Murillo "Grape and Melon Eaters", Velázquez "Young Spanish Nobleman".

Cabinets

1—2: Giotto "The Last Supper", Fra Angelico "The Legend of St. Cosmas and Damian", among others

3: Barbari "Still Life", Mantegna "Mucius Scaevola"

4: Leonardo da Vinci "Mary with Child"

5: Vecchio "Mary with Child, St. Rochus and Magdelen"

6: Liss "Cleopatra"

7: van Dyck "Lamentation of Christ"

8: Rubens "Medici Cycle"

9: Rubens "Susanna at the Bath"

10: Adriaen Brouwer

11: Adam Elsheimer, Georg Flegel, Johann Rottenhammer

12: Rubens, among others, "Battle of the Amazons", "The Fall of the Damned to Hell"

14: Jan van Goyen, Pieter Claesz, Willem Kalf

15: Pieter Lastmann

16: Rembrandt, among others, "A Representation from the Passion"

17: Adraen van Ostade

18: Jacob van Ruisdael, Meindert Hobbema

19: Gerard Terborch, Nicolas Berchem

20: Philips Wouverman, Pieter van Laer

21—22: Jan Steen, Willem Kalf, Emanuel de Witte

23: Giovanni Tiepolo, Rosalba Carriera.

The paintings displayed on the *ground floor* in the east wing are mainly concerned with sacred themes, with the exception of room IIa, which contains four portraits from the late Gothic, Dürer, and early Renaissance periods. The west wing houses Dutch paintings from the 16th and 17th centuries.

Early German School (rooms I—III, cabinets 1—10): among others, the Master of the Polling Panels, Hans Pleydenwurf "Hofer Altarpiece", Lucas Cranach the Elder "Adam and Eve" and "St. Anna with Mary and the child Jesus", Michael Pacher "Altar of the Church Fathers" and "Panels from the Laurentius Altar", Hans Burgkmaier the Elder "St. John's Altar" and "Cross Altar", Hans Holbein the Elder "Kaisheim Altarpiece", Stephan Lochner "Adoration of Christ". – Stephan Lochner, Master of St. Veronica, Master of the Life of the Virgin, Bartholomäus Bryn the Elder, Master of the Holy Family, Master of Bartholomew Altar.

European Painting of the 16th and 17th Centuries (rooms XII—XIII, cabinets 19—23): among others David Teniers the Younger "Fair in front of the Church", Giorgio Vasari "The Holy Family with St. John", Lucas Cranach the Elder "The Suicide of Lucretia", Paul Bril "The Tower of Babel", Hans van Aachen, Friedrich Sustris. – Jan Brueghel the Elder "Troy Burning", Pieter Brueghel the Elder "Fool's Paradise".

North of the Alte Pinakothek is the

**NEUE PINAKOTHEK [70]

The foundation of the New Pinakothek also was laid by Ludwig I in 1846, who wanted to have a building for works of art "of his time". The construction was carried out by the architect August von Voit, based on plans by Friedrich von Gärtner. In the Second World War the building was damaged so badly that the construction of a new building was decided on. In 1966 a contest of ideas was organized, which was won by the Munich architect Alexander von Branca. The official opening of the new building took place in March 1981.

The entrance hall displays works by Carl Rottmann on the right side. Rooms A and B are reserved for changing exhibitions.

The numbers of the following survey are in accordance with the official numbering of the rooms.

1–2a: International art about 1800 (David, Gainsborough, Canova, Goya, Turner, and others)

3–3a: Early Romantic painters (Blechen, Friedrich, Dahl, Rottmann, Kobell, Kersting, Dillis)

4–4a: Court art under Ludwig I (Stieler, Catel, P. von Hess, Thorvaldsen, Rebell, Wittmer, Bürkel)

5–5a: German neo-classical painters in Rome (Koch, Reinhart, Hackert, Fries)

6: Collection Georg Schäfer

7: Nazarene (Overbeck, W. von Schadow, Olivier, H. Hess)

8–9: Biedermeier (Schwind, Quaglio, Adam, Waldmüller, Amerling, Alt)

10–10a: French Late Romanticists and Realists (Gérecault, Corot, Courbet, Millet, Daumier, Corot, Delacroix)

11–11a: German Late Romanticists and Realists (Menzel, Achenbach, Rayski, Spitzweg, Schleich, Volz)

12: Kaulbach's designs for the outward frescoes of the Neue Pinakothek

13–13a: Historical and social painting (Piloty, Winterhalter, H. Vernet, Gallait, Riedel)

14–14a: Painting from the "Gründerzeit", the time of industrial expansion about 1870 (Defregger, Munkascy, Markart, Schleich, Wenglein, Max, Keller, Lenbach)

15: Hans von Marées

16: Böcklin, Feuerbach, Thoma

17: Leibl and his circle (Schuch, Trübner)

18: French Impressionists (Manet, Monet, Degas, Pissaro, Renoir)

19: Cézanne, van Gogh, Gauguin, Rogin

20: Social Realism (Liebermann, Slevogt, Uhde, Meunier)

21: German Impressionism (Corinth, Slevogt, Zügel)

21a: Secessionists (Putz, Habermann, Dill, Overbeck)

22–22a: Symbolism and Art Nouveau (Klinger, Klimt, Hodler, Stuck, Khnopff, Toulouse-Lautrec, Vuillard, Bonnard, Denis, Signac).

Mineralogische Staatssammlung [71]

This museum of mineralogy in Theresienstraße (entrance Barer Straße opposite the Alte Pinakothek) contains interesting collections from the world of minerals and cristals.

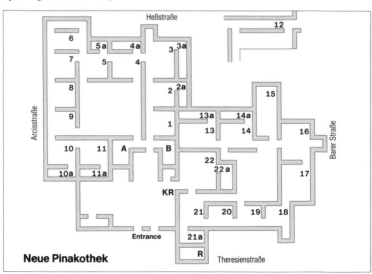

Setting down new standards of urban plannings was not only restricted to King *Maximilian I,* who had designed the Max-Vorstadt, or to *Ludwig I,* who had himself built an architectural monument in the neo-classical Ludwigstraße. Concepts for the extension of the city were commissioned by the succeeding rulers as well: So King *Maximilian II* ordered the construction of Maximilianstraße and Prince Regent *Luitpold* the long west-east axis of Prinzregentenstraße, already planned by Ludwig II, but not carried out. Both of these splendid streets viewed as ensembles have become typical parts of Munich.

*MAXIMILIANSTRASSE

In 1852 King Maximilian II (reigned 1848–1864) had the construction of Maximilianstraße begun under the supervision of *Friedrich Bürklein* (1813–1872). As the king put it "a style representing the culture of these days" was to be discovered, which later on found its place in art history as "Maximilian style". It incorporates a synthesis of various architectural forms with a marked tendency for the vertical structuring typical of Gothic art. The street was planned as a connection between the city centre and the large greens of the Isar meadows. The king decided on a strictly structured street system at the beginning of the boulevard, which then opens and stretches broadly and parklike down to the Isar. Modern traffic planning, however, spoiled the organic structure of this splendid boulevard, when the Altstadtring was inconsiderately laid across it.

The starting point for Maximilianstraße is *Max-Joseph-Platz* with the loggia of the Post Office Nr. 1 by Leo von Klenze and the National Theatre. Opposite the opera there is a row of commercial buildings, designed by Friedrich Bürklein in 1859–1863.

The building of the hotel *Vier Jahreszeiten* [72] was constructed in 1856–1858 by Rudolf Wilhelm Gottgetreu, a pupil of Karl Friedrich Schinkel, who had been offered a professor's chair at the then Technical Academy by Maximilian I. On the other side of the street is the *Schauspielhaus* [73] or playhouse. The building of the Kammerspiele was erected by Max Littmann and Richard Riemerschmid in 1900–1901 in Art Nouveau. After its destruction in the Second World War, it was rebuilt according to the original plans, thus providing the city of Munich with one of the few pure Art Nouveau theatres in the German Federal Republik.

Not far to the east of the Schauspielhaus Maximilianstraße widens out like a forum. On the left is the building of the

Regierung von Oberbayern [74]

the Government of Upper Bavaria. It is one of the most outstanding examples of the "Maximilian style". This edifice, strongly influenced by English Gothic, was built in 1856–1864 by Friedrich Bürklein. Above the ground floor, with its arcades, are neo-Gothic arches of a markedly vertical character. The main building with its 17 axes is flanked right and left by 5-axled and 3-axled additions. Opposite the government building is the

Völkerkundemuseum [75]

The Ethnological Museum, also greatly influenced by English Gothic, was erected by Eduard Riedel in 1858–1865. The museum, the first exhibits of which had been collected by Ludwig I, possesses a fine collection of cultural items from non-European countries from all over the world. In particular *works of art and objects of everyday use from Africa, East Asia, Oceania and Latin America* are represented. Special exhibitions enable the house to make its comprehensive collection accessible to the public from time to time.

Displays from other exhibitions and lectures complete the cultural program of the museum.

In the park between the two last-mentioned buildings are bronze statues, created between 1858 and 1863: on the north side are the Bavarian general *Count Deroy* (1743–1812) and the "father" of the English Garden, *Count Rumford* (Benjamin Thompson, 1753–1814); on the south side are statues of the philosopher *Friedrich Wilhelm Schelling* (1775–1854) and the physicist and astronomer *Joseph Fraunhofer* (1787–1826).

49

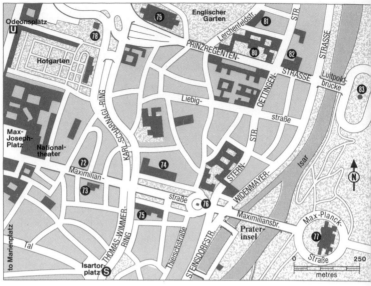

At the centre of the forum Maximilianstraße is the

Max-Monument [76]

Kaspar von Zumbusch created this monument in 1875 in memory of King Maximilian II, who furthered art, science and social progress. The people of Munich call it for short "Max Zwo" (Max Two). The four great sitting bronze figures are allegorical representations of the four virtues of a ruler, the four putti bear the coat of arms of the four Bavarian tribes: the Bavarians, the Franconians, the Swabians, and the people of the Palatinate.

The Isar is spanned by the *Maximiliansbrücke* or bridge. On a high pedestal stands the statue of *Pallas Athene,* symbolizing Munich as a city of art.

Looking up from the Maximilianstraße to the other bank of the Isar, we cannot fail to notice the

Maximilianeum [77]

The foundation stone to the edifice was laid by Friedrich Bürklein in 1857, who, however, did not live to see the completion of the building in 1874. Through Gottfried Semper's influence Renaissance forms were introduced into the pointed-arch architecture of Bürklein.

According to the royal foundation document the Maximilianeum originally had only the purpose of offering the best youths in the country free and adequate accomodation, thus enabling them to complete their studies and training for high state posts without any financial worries. Since 1949 the Maximilianeum has been the home of the *Bavarian Landtag,* or parliament, and its *Senate,* the advisory second chamber. For these institutions extensions (with committee rooms, a swimming pool, etc.) were built to the east in 1957−1960.

The inner rooms, still partly decorated with frescoes, are not open to the public. The balustrade in front of the Maximilianeum, however, is open to visitors and offers a great view of the city of Munich and the parks along the banks of the river Isar.

PRINZREGENTENSTRASSE

The last great urban extension in the 19th century was Prinzregentenstraße, the construction of which was begun in 1890. Though lacking architectural unity, it nevertheless radiates the spirit of the turn of the century, despite numerous rebuildings.

At the beginning of the street stands a building from an earlier era, the

Prinz-Carl-Palais [78]

built by Carl von Fischer in early neo-classical style for the minister Abbé von Salabert. As of 1825 it served as residence for Prince Carl (died 1875). In 1826 Jean-Baptist Métivier extended the western part of the building. In 1937 F. Gablonsky partly rebuilt the edifice in a very elegant fashion.

The porticus protrudes unusually far from the nine-axled east façade. Its triple vertical subdivision emphasizes the strict symmetry of the building. The Prince Carl Palace is the most beautiful early neo-classical building in Munich. Its architectural effect, however, has suffered considerably from traffic projects: the Altstadtring (city circuit) passes nearby and the Prinzregentenstraße goes under the building itself. Today the palace serves as a *seat of representation for the Bavarian minister-president.* Some of its rooms are part of the *Bavarian State Chancellery.*

On the opposite, left hand side of Prinz-regentenstraße, stands the

**Haus der Kunst [79]

The House of Art was erected in 1933–1937 as a substitute for the Glass Palace in the Old Botanical Garden, which burnt down in 1931. It was built by Paul Ludwig Troost in the monumental style typical of the Third Reich. While changing exhibitions are held in the east wing and the middle part of the 145-metre-long neo-classical building the west wing houses the

Staatsgalerie Moderner Kunst (State Gallery of Modern Art, see p. 12). The emphasis here is placed on collection of contemporary works of art:

2: Early Expressionism (Matisse, Picasso, Braque, Munch)
3: Ernst Ludwig Kirchner
4: "Die Brücke" (Heckel, Schmidt-Rotluff, Nolde, Pechstein, Mueller)
5–6: Cubism (Braque, Picasso, Gris, Chagall, Leger)
7–8: "Der Blaue Reiter" (Kandinsky, Marc, Macke, Münter, Jawlensky)
9: Corinth, Kokoschka, Schiele
10: Max Beckmann
11: Surrealism and pittura metafisica (de Chirico, Dali, Ernst, Magritta, Miró)
12: Paul Klee
13: Bauhaus (Feininger, Kandinsky, Schlemmer)
14: New Functualism (Carrà, Davringhausen, Dix, Hubbuch, Kanoldt)
15: Late Expressionism (Rohlfs, Kirchner, Hofer, König)
16–16a: Sophie and Emanuel Fohn Donation (Beckmann, Macke, Marc, Kokoschka)
17: Abstract German Painting (Baumeister, Kandinsky, Nay)
18: Late Picasso and Moore
19: Abstract German Painting from the Post-war Period (Baumeister, Bissier, Nay, Werner, Winter)
20: International Abstract Painting (Hartung, Poliakoff, Soulages)
21: Marino Marini (donation by the artist)

First Floor (North)

22: Fruhtrunk
23–24: Op Art
25: Minimal Art

First Floor (South)

26: American Abstract Expressionism (de Kooning, Johns, Louis)
27: "Cobra" Group
28: Abstract Painting
29: Material Pictures (Burri, Beuys, Dubuffet, Tapies)

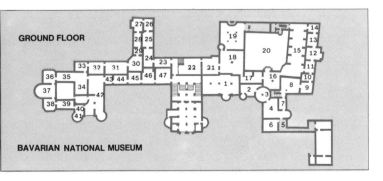

51

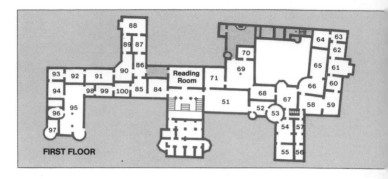

FIRST FLOOR

30: Pop Art (Christo, Oldenbourg, Rauschenberg, Segal, Warhol)
31: Botera and Richter
32: Antes and Baselitz
33: Comtemporary Realists (Asmus, Gertsch, Klapheck, Nagel)

Further east on the left side of Prinz-regentenstraße (beyond Lerchenfeld-straße) is the

**BAYERISCHES NATIONALMUSEUM [80]

The building of the Bavarian National Museum was erected by Gabriel von Seidl in 1894—1900. Even the museum's exterior mirrors the various art periods represented in it: the east wing the Romanic period, the west wing the Renaissance, the middle section with its tower the early baroque and the building to the west the rococo.

In front of the east wing is an *equestrian statue of Prince Regent Luitpold,* designed by Adolf von Hildebrand in 1901—1903.

The collections of the museum date back to an exhibition arranged by Maximilian II in the Herzog-Max-Burg in 1855. They are divided into two main groups: the *art historical collection* and the *folklore collection* (for opening hours see p. 12).

Ground Floor

Rooms 1—18: Middle Ages. The following rooms deserve special attention: 1 (Wessobrunn room), 2 (Room of the Virgin with the rose bush), 4 (Bamberg room), 8 (Multscher room), 11 (Füssen room), 13 (Room of Flemish tapestry), 15 (Room of churches), 16 (Riemenschneider room), 17 (Late Gothic, c. 1500), 18 (Hall of Armour).

Rooms 19—30: Renaissance. The following rooms are particularly important: 21 (Leinberger room), 22 (German Renaissance), 23 (Italian Renaissance), 25 (Paulaner chapel), 26 (Late Italian Renaissance), 28 (Laiunger room), 29 (Late German Renaissance), 30 (Wilhelm V room).

Rooms 31—43: Baroque and Rococo. The following rooms are especially notable: 31 (Maximilian room), 32 (Henriette Adelaide room), 33 and 34 (Max-Emanuel rooms), 38 (Religious craftsmanship in the 18th century), 42 and 43 (Ignaz Günther rooms).

Rooms 44—46: Classicism. Of particular interest are the two King's rooms.

Room 47: Jakob Sandtner's models of Bavarian towns.

First floor

Rooms 53 and 54: Collection Wilhelm Reuschel.
Rooms 58 and 59: Clocks, watches and automatons.
Rooms 67 and 68: Rococo costumes.
Room 70: Schwanthaler room.
Rooms 84—87 and 98—100: Porcelain.
Rooms 92—95: Faience.

Basement

Rooms 101—131: Folk art. Especially worthy of note are rooms 101—109 (peasant interiors), 110—117 (religious folklore), 128—131 (costumes and ornamentation).
*East Basement: *Collection of cribs.* The cribs 1—9 and 21—34 are from Bavaria, Austria and Moravia, the cribs 35—52 from Northern, Middle and Southern Italy (Naples), the cribs 50A, 52, 55—63 from Southern Italy and Sicily.

Behind the National Museum in *Lerchenfeldstraße* is the modern building of the

*Prähistorische Staatssammlung [81]

The Prehistoric State Collection provides information about the cultural periods in Bavaria from Paleolithic times up to the early Middle Ages. Changing exhibitions with prehistoric and culturally important historic items are held here as well (for opening hours see p. 12).

The permanent exhibition is divided into the following cultural periods:

Stone Age (room 1), Bronze Age (up to the 13th century B.C., room 2), Urn Field Age (up to the 8th century B.C., room 3), Hallstatt Age (up to 500 B.C., room 4), Latène Age (up to 15 B.C., room 5), Manching (settlement of the late Latène Age, room 6), Roman Era I–III (rooms 7–9), Alamans, Bavarians, Franconians (5th to 7th century, room 10), Merovingian and Carolingian Eras (room 11), early Middle Ages up to the founding of Munich (room 12).

Following Prinzregentenstraße towards the Isar, we come to the building of the

*Schackgalerie [82]

Commissioned by Emperor Wilhelm II, it was erected by Max Littmann in 1907–1909 in connection with the Prussian Embassy Building (today the Bavarian State Chancellery). In the second half of the 19th century Adolf Friedrich von Schack (1815–1894), a former Prussian state official, had collected numerous masterpieces of contemporary artists. For this reason Wilhelm II bestowed upon him the title of count. In his will Schack left his collection to the emperor, who, however, insisted that the paintings should remain in the city of Munich.

The former private collection of the art-patron Schack, which was incorporated in the Bavarian State Picture Collection in 1939, includes paintings from the early Romantic period (Dillis, Klenze), works by Carl Rottmann up to paintings by Moritz von Schwindt, Carl Spitzweg, Anselm Feuerbach, Franz von Lenbach, Arnold Böcklin, and Hans von Marées (for opening hours see p. 12).

Crossing *Prinzregentenbrücke* or bridge, we encounter a work of art dominating the park along the Isar, the

Friedensengel [82]

The Angel of Peace Monument, donated by the city of Munich in 1896 in remembrance of the preliminary peace of Versailles and in gratitude to the Bavarian army, consists of a terrace in Florentine style and a 23-metre-high column.

The terrace is the work of Adolf von Hildebrand and Jakob Möhl. The column was designed by Joseph Bühlmann (architect), Heinrich Düll, Max Heilmaier, and Georg Pezold (sculptors).

Angel of Peace Monument

The angel, six metres high, on the fluted shaft of the column with Corinthian capital, is meant to resemble the goddess of victory (Nike) in Olympia.

Farther east in Prinzregentenstraße (Nr. 60) is the

Stuckvilla

It was built in 1897–1898 according to plans of the owner, the "painter prince" Franz von Stuck (1863–1923). The interior decoration of the house is a prime example of Art Nouveau (original frescoes, painting, graphic drawings and documentation from about 1900). Today the building also houses various galleries. The *bronze figure* in front of the neo-classical main entrance, a spear-throwing Amazon, is based on a design by Stuck himself.

About 300 metres further east at *Prinzregentenplatz* is the

Prinzregententheater

The Prince Regent's Theatre was constructed in 1899–1901 according to the draft of Gottfried Semper for the Wagner festival theatre planned by Ludwig II. The theatre is at present vacant.

53

9th Walk. The West:
Theresienwiese – Messegelände – Westpark

From the *main railway station* (U- and S-Bahn) we follow *Bayerstraße* in a westerly direction and turn left into *Hermann-Lingg-Straße*.

Before we get to Bavariaring we see the *Parish Church St. Paul* [84] to the left. The basilica with its three aisles was built in neo-Gothic style between 1892 and 1906 by Georg Joseph von Haubenrisser. *Bavariaring* forms the eastern flank of the

Theresienwiese [85]

or meadow. Its history dates back to a horse race held on October 17th, 1810, in honour of the wedding of Crown Prince Ludwig and Therese von Sachsen-Hildburghausen. The memory of the folk festival simultaneously held is still kept alive by the *Oktoberfest*.

The west flank of the Theresienwiese is dominated by the

Bavaria and the Ruhmeshalle [86]

Including its base, the monument of the *Bavaria* is about 30 m high. The bronze statue itself measures 15.8 metres. The design for the bronze figure was by Schwanthaler, the figure was cast by Ferdinand von Miller in 1844–1850. The

Bavaria can be climbed from the inside by a spiral staircase (130 steps). Five small openings in the head offer a splendid view of the city *(open daily, except Mondays, 10–12 a.m. and 2–4 p.m.)*.

Ludwig I commissioned not only the Bavaria, but also the *Ruhmeshalle* or Hall of Fame. Between 1843 and 1853 Leo von Klenze built this open colonnade hall with its protruding corner risalite in Dorian style to honour deserving Bavarians.

Behind the Bavaria on the *Theresienhöhe* or heights extends the

Messegelände [87]

The Exhibition Park covers about 330,000 sq. m with twenty pavilions. More than 30 international fairs and exhibitions attract about 1.2 million visitors yearly to Munich.

The newly created **Westpark,** further southwest in Untersendling and crossed by the Garmischer Straße, is the scene for the *International Horticultural Exhibition 1983* (new underground station Westpark of the U 3 and U 6). The exhibition area, 73 hectars large, presents outdoor gardens and indoor exhibitions with plants from all the world, floating stage, restaurants and cafés.

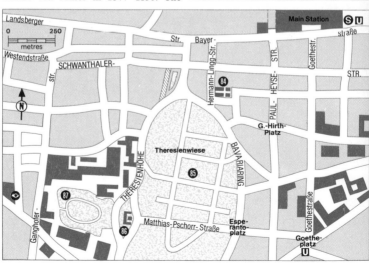

Schloß and Schloßpark Nymphenburg

Schloß Nymphenburg or Nymphenburg Palace is about 8 kilometres from the centre of Munich and can be reached with the 17 or 21 tram and the 41 bus.

Opening hours: The park is open daily from 6 a.m. until dusk. The palace and other buildings (with the exception of the Amalienburg) are closed Mondays. The palace and the Amalienburg are open in the summer months (April 1st — September 30th) 9 a.m. — 12.30 p.m. and 1.30–5 p.m., and in the winter season 10 a.m. — 12.30 p.m. and 1.30–4 p.m. The Badenburg, Pagodenburg and Magdalenenklause are open only in summer from 10 a.m. — 12.30 p.m. and 1.30–5 p.m. The Marstallmuseum is open daily in summer 9–12 a.m. and 1–5 p.m., and in winter 10–12 a.m. and 1–4 p.m., except Mondays. To visit all the buildings (with a collective ticket) an admission charge must be paid.

**Schloß Nymphenburg

or Nymphenburg Palace. Out of gratitude for the birth of his heir Max Emanuel, Elector Ferdinand Maria gave his wife Henriette Adelaide of Savoy the *Schwaige* or dairy farm, west of Munich. At first the centre building with its double flight of outdoor steps was erected, to serve as summer residence of the Wittelsbachs. In 1664 Agostino Barelli began this work, which was continued by Enrico Zuccalli as of 1673. In 1675 the centre building was completed.

In 1702–1704, during the reign of Elector Maximilian II Emanuel, Antonio Viscardi added the four cubic pavilions, connecting them with the central building by arcades according to plan by Zuccalli; the two eastern pavilions were not finished before 1716 by Joseph Effner.

In 1719 the palace was extended again. To the south the *Marstall* (stables) was built and in 1723–1724 to the north – as a counterpart – the four-winged complex of the *Orangerie* was erected, both with their connecting buildings. The garden pavilions also date from these years. François Cuvilliés was commissioned by Elector Karl Albrecht to design the great *crescent* in front of the palace (1729–1758), with the houses of the court officials (in the middle building in the northeast of the semi-circle the *Nymphenburg Porcelain Manufactory*, founded in 1747, was housed).

Maximilian III Joseph limited himself to rebuilding the palace on the inside. Thus in 1755–1757 he had given the great hall, the "Steinerner Saal", its present splendour through the work of Cuvilliés and Johann Baptist Zimmermann.

The *Steinerner Saal,* the two-storied festive hall of the centre building goes back

Nymphenburg Palace

to plans by Enrico Zuccalli and Joseph Effner. The ceiling frescoes are by Johann Baptist Zimmermann.

The former *Kleiner Speisesaal* or small dining room (south pavilion) became Ludwig I's famous *Schönheitsgalerie* or Gallery of Beauties, painted by Josef Stieler between 1827 and 1850. It includes a painting of the dancer Lola Montez, whose affair with the king was one of the reasons for Ludwig I's abdication in 1848.

In the second, northern pavilion the *Schloßkapelle* or Palace Chapel is worth seeing. The Chapel of St. Magdalen was built according to drafts by Antonio Viscardi and consecrated in 1715. The ceiling fresco is by Joseph Mölck. The statue of Christ is attributed to Andreas Faistenberger.

**Schloßpark Nymphenburg

or Palace Park Nymphenburg. In front of the west façade of the palace spreads forth the so-called *Great Parterre,* the only remembrance of the former French garden. One's view passes from the straight middle axis (decorated on both sides with stone sculptures of Greek gods) to the main canal with a *cascade* at the end, which was built by Dominique

Girard in 1731 according to plans by Joseph Effner. What was originally an Italian garden (1671) was later turned into a French and baroque park and finally transformed into a great English park of 221 hectars by Friedrich Ludwig Sckell in 1803–1805. There are several pavilions scattered over this park. Left of the Great Parterre is the

**Amalienburg, a hunting lodge built by Elector Karl Albrecht for his wife Maria Amalia. This palace, erected in 1734–1739, is a masterpiece of Cuvilliés' rococo. Around the centre of the building, the round *Spiegelsaal* or Hall of Mirrors, several rooms are clustered, such as the *Blue Cabinet* (the bedroom of the Electress), the *Hunting Room* (with rifle cabinets above the kennels of the pack of hounds) and the *Pheasant Room.*

Deeper within the park and also on the left side of the canal, we come to the

*Badenburg, built by Joseph Effner from 1718–1721 in French style. The rich stucco ornamentation was the work of Charles Claude Debut. The lodge took its name from a large *room for bathing* with a heated pool, which Elector Maximilian II Emanuel had constructed here.

On the other side of the *Badenburger See* or Badenburg Lake is the *Temple of Apollo.* At the *cascade* we cross the middle axis and turn southeast, thus reaching at the *Kleiner See* (the "little lake") the

*Pagodenburg, erected in octagonal form by Joseph Effner in 1716–1719.

François Cuvilliés renewed the façade and the interior decorations in 1767. The little palace took its name from the pagodas painted by Johann Anton Gumpp on the ceiling of the upper storey (Chinese style).

Further east, towards Nymphenburg Palace, we come to the

Magdalenenklause or Magdalen's Hermitage, which Maximilian II Emanuel had built as a hermitage for himself. Effner erected this artificial ruin with grotto chapel in 1725. The stucco statue of St. Magdalen was the work of Guiseppe Volponi (1726). The ceiling painting was created by Nikolaus Gottfried Stuber.

Leaving the park and turning right we come to the

*Marstallmuseum or Royal Stables Museum, located in the south wing of Nymphenburg Palace. In the former coachhouse of the Wittelsbachs are now kept state coaches, sledges, harnesses and riding equipment.

Botanischer Garten
The Botanical Gardens (17 and 21 trams) immediately adjoin Nymphenburg Park. They were laid out between 1909 and 1914 and contain a fine collection of orchids, cacti and cycadaceae, as well as special sections devoted to *alpine flora* and rhododendrons. *Open: Grounds, summer 9 a.m. – 7 p.m.; winter 9 a.m. – 5 p.m. Greenhouses 9–11.45 a.m. and 1–6.30 p.m. in summer; winter same and 1–4.30 p.m. Admission fee.*

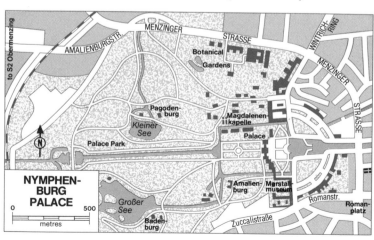

Sights on the City Outskirts

CHURCHES

*Schloßkapelle Blutenburg in Obermenzing (73 bus from Nymphenburg). Duke Sigismund had the Blutenburg Castle Chapel erected, a splendid masterpiece of late Gothic style, in 1488 next to the former moated castle (also late Gothic, see p. 58). On the inside the *stained-glass windows,* the three *altar paintings* (Holy Trinity, Christ with crown and globe, and the Annunciation) by Jan Polack (1491), as well as the *limewood figures* of Christ, the Virgin and the 12 apostles are worth seeing. *(Open daily 2–5 p.m.)*

St. Martin in Untermenzing (76 bus from Blutenburg). Like Blutenburg Castle Chapel this late Gothic church was donated by Duke Sigismund. In this church, built by Ulrich Randeck in 1499, the six Gothic *stained-glass windows* (1499) and the *paintings of the high altar* (beginning of the 17th century) are of particular interest.

Pfarrkirche St. Wolfgang in Pipping (Pippinger Straße 49a; 10 minutes by foot from Blutenburg Castle). The Parish Church of St. Wolfgang was also built under Duke Sigismund, but ten years before he commissioned the construction of Blutenburg Castle Chapel. This late Gothic treasure, erected in 1478, has survived almost unaltered and undamaged. Jan Polack created the *paintings* in the chancel and on the walls (1479). The *stained-glass windows* date from the year 1478. The three *carved altars* dating from the period when the church was built are worth mentioning. The artists are unknown.

Pfarrkirche St. Ulrich in Laim (Agnes-Bernauer-Straße 104; 19 and 29 trams, S-Bahn 1 and 2). The Parish Church St. Ulrich goes back to a chapel of the 11th century, belonging to a large estate. The choir and the tower are 15th century late Gothic.

St. Georg in Bogenhausen (Neuberghauser Straße; 18 and 20 trams). This baroque church, built by Johann Michael Fischer in 1759, is situated in the middle of an idyllic churchyard, where well-known Munich citizens, including Liesl Karlstadt, Erich Kästner and Hans Knappersbusch, were laid to rest. Originally a Romanesque construction had stood here. The *frescoes,* completed in 1770, were the work of Philipp Helterhof, the *high altar* with St. George on horseback is by Johann Baptist Straub, the *pulpit* and the right *side altar* are by Ignaz Günther.

*Hofkirche St. Michael in Berg am Laim (U 8). The Court Church of St. Michael in its present form was built under the Prince Bishop Clemens August of Cologne, nephew of Elector Maximilian II Emanuel, by Johann Michael Fischer between 1738 and 1751. An earlier little church, donated by Clemens August's uncle, Prince Bishop Joseph Clemens, to the Order honouring the Archangel Michael, had become too small in the course of time. The *stucco* and *frescoes* were created by Johann Baptist Zimmermann in 1743, the *side altars* (1743–1759) as well as the *high altar* (1767) were constructed by Johann Baptist Strauß. The pulpit was the work of Benedikt Haßler (1745).

St. Stephan in Berg am Laim (Baumkirchner Straße 45; S-Bahn 4 and 6). According to documents this church is probably the oldest in Munich. Already before the city was founded it was part of the imperial possessions until 1052, when it passed over to the bishop of Freising. The late Gothic church building was erected by Lukas Rottaler about 1510. The interior was done in baroque style in 1713.

Pfarrkirche St. Maria in Ramersdorf (Aribonenstraße 9; U-Bahn 8 to Karl-Preis-Platz, then bus 95). As early as the 14th century the Parish Church of St. Mary was one of the favourite places of pilgrimage in Old Bavaria. The church, dating back to the 11th century, was replaced by a new construction in Gothic style at the beginning of the 15th century and had baroque elements added in 1675. Inside the **Virgin on the high altar* and the **representation of the Crucifixion on the wing altar* (Erasmus Grasser, about 1510), the *paintings* of Jan Polack (1483) on the wing altar as well as a *votary picture* of the 42 hostages taken by Gustavus Adolphus of Sweden (Matthias Kager, 1635) are worth noticing.

Pfarrkirche St. Maria in Thalkirchen (Frauenbergplatz 1; 31 and 57 buses).

The Parish Church of St. Mary, which was probably founded in the 14th century, acquired its baroque form in 1692 and was expanded by Gabriel von Seidl in 1906. The *high altar* with its late Gothic miraculous image by Gregor Erhart (1482) was given its present form by Ignaz Günther.

Pfarrkirche Heilig Kreuz in Forstenried (Forstenrieder Allee 180a; 66 bus from Harras). The single-aisled late Gothic building of the Parish Church Holy Cross (beginning of the 15th century) was redone in baroque style on the inside by Gasparo Zuccalli. The high altar is decorated with a late Romanesque *wooden crucifix,* which was probably carved about 1200 in the monastery at Seeon.

St. Johann Baptist in Johanneskirchen (Gleißenbachstraße 2; S-Bahn 3). The main part of this little village church goes back to the 13th century. The *frescoes* on the north wall are from the 14th century, the *portal* dates from 1520. In 1688 a new ceiling vault with stucco was installed. The *high altar* with statues by Ignaz Günther is worth seeing.

St. Lorenz in Oberföhring (Muspillistraße 14; 88 and 188 buses). Wolfgang Zwerger built this church in 1680. The *high altar* is from the same year. Beautiful stucco work.

PALACES

Asam-Schlößchen (Benediktbeurer Straße 19; 31 and 57 buses and a 10 minutes walk; 62 and 66 buses from Harras). The sculptor and painter Cosmas Damian Asam, after whom this little palace is called, rebuilt the country seat in "Maria Einsiedel" as a residence for himself in 1729—1732.

Blutenburg (Obermenzing; 73 bus from Nymphenburg). Already before the time of Duke Sigismund was a hunting lodge here, built by Duke Albrecht III in 1439. At that time the late Gothic building was still surrounded by the Würm river. During the Thirty Years' War it was partially burnt down. In 1681 the palace was rebuilt. Right now, however, the building is temporarily closed; it is being redone to house the *International Youth Library.*

Fürstenried (Forst-Kasten-Allee; 34 bus from Pasing). Commissioned by Elector

Maximilian II Emanuel, Joseph Effner built this former hunting lodge in 1715—1717, which later on served as a place of residence for the Electress Anna Maria from 1778 to 1796. The symmetrically laid out complex is oriented straight towards the Frauenkirche (8 km away) by an alley of lime trees.

Suresnes-Schlößchen (Werneckstraße 1, Schwabing). In 1715—1718 Johann Baptist Gunezrhainer built this little palace, then still located in the suburbs, for a cabinet secretary.

**OLYMPIAPARK

The sport and recreation area of the Olympia Park comprising 2.8 sq.km was laid out at the occasion of the 20th Olympic Summer Games in 1972. On the site of *Oberwiesenfeld,* the former royal Bavarian parade ground, construction of buildings and sport facilities was begun in 1966. The "Schuttberg" (a hill built out of the rubble of the houses destroyed in Munich during the Second World War) was also included. It is the present 60-metre-high *Olympiaberg.*

The Fernsehturm (Television Tower), as symbol for the Olympic Summer Games also called *Olympiaturm* or

Tent roof and Olympia tower

tower, is almost 290 m high and overtops the whole complex. The tower's upper platform has an observation terrace and a revolving restaurant (lift fee 3 DM, daily 9 a.m. — 12 p.m.) from where you get a splendid view of the city; on days with Föhn (see p. 4) even the distant Alps seem to be within reach.

Olympiastadion and **Zeltdach. Olympic Stadium and Tent Roof are designs by the architect association Behnisch and partners (1968−1972). The *Olympic Stadium* can hold about 80,000 people.

The *Olympic Sports Hall* built as a multipurpose hall can hold up to 4,000 visitors at stage performances and up to 14,000 people at boxing matches. The hall is also used for six-day bicycle races and large Fasching parties.

With its costs of construction of 165 million marks the 74,800-square-metre **Zeltdach or Tent Roof was the most expensive one in the world. The construction consists of a tubular network, covered with transparent plastic "tiles" of acryll-glass, hung from 12 mats up to 80 metres high.

The *Eissporthalle* or Ice Stadium (7,000 spectators) at the entrance of the Olympia Park was built by R. Schütze. The *Radsportstadion* or Cycle Stadium (5,000 spectators) at the end of the park was erected by H. Schürmann.

To the south of the sport facilities is the *Olympiasee* (Olympia Lake), an artificial lake deriving its water from the Nymphenburg canal. The *Theatron* is also located here (a floating stage with its auditorium on the bank of the lake). It is used for open-air concerts (especially pop music). Southwest of the Olympiaberg amidst a once well cultivated garden there stands a *Russian Orthodox chapel*. It was built after the Second World War by a Russian recluse, known as "Väterchen Timofy" ("Father Timofy").

The Olympische Dörfer or Olympic Villages are north of the Mittlerer Ring. The high rise buildings formed the *village for men,* designed by the architect association Heinle, Wischer and partners in 1968−1972. The low buildings were the *village for women,* created by Eckert and Wirsing in 1969−1971. While the high rise apartments of the village for men have been sold as owner-occupied flats, the village for women after the Olympic Games was turned into a "city for students", housing about 1800 students.

Directly beside the Olympic grounds, the *administrative tower of the Bavarian Motor Works (BMW)* rises almost 100 m high. Next to it there is the bowl-shaped concrete building of the *BMW-Museum* (see p. 12; a collection of aircraft engines, motor-cycles and motor-cars of the Bavarian Motor Works from 1919 to the present in a modern representation).

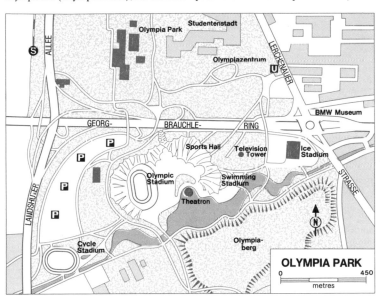

OLYMPIA PARK

0   450
metres

*TIERPARK HELLABRUNN

(Siebenbrunner Straße; 57 bus from Sendlinger Tor, 52 bus from Marienplatz). *Open in summer from 8 a.m. to 6 p.m., in winter from 9 a.m. to 5 p.m. The animal houses are closed about half an hour earlier. Admission charge.*

Hellabrunn Zoo was laid out in 1911 according to plans by Emanuel Seidl under the patronage of Prince Regent Luitpold. Its name dates back to a mansion once located here. In 1928 Heinz Heck, zoologist and director of the zoo, gave the complex its present form. The grounds cover 70 hectars.

Hellabrunn Zoo is the only "geographical zoo" in the world. That means, the animals here are arranged according to their continent of origin (Europe, America, Australia, Africa, Asia and the polar regions). An attempt has been made to reproduce specific climatic regions, thus providing the animals the most comfortable homelike conditions.

This method has had considerable success. The Munich zoo is the only zoo with an excess of births over deaths.

The only enclosure housing animals from all continents is the *large aviary* for about 200 birds, which was opened in 1980. The architectural layout of this 5000 sq. m wire-netted complex is by Jörg Giebl. Animals of special interest in this zoo are the *bison, white-tailed gnu, ibex, onaga, wild banteng* and *Père David's deer.*

Especially popular is the *anthropoid ape section,* which breeds more chimpanzees than any other zoo in Europa. In this section you can also find the world famous orangoutan twins Hella and Bruno (born February 2nd 1969), the first orangoutans born in a zoo. Other superlative attractions are the *grounds for polar animals,* the largest in Europe, and an *aquarium* with about 40 basins for aquatic animals from all parts of the world.

A special attraction for children is the *Kinderzoo* (children's zoo) with ponies, and dwarf species of donkeys, monkeys, goats – all to be touched and cuddled.

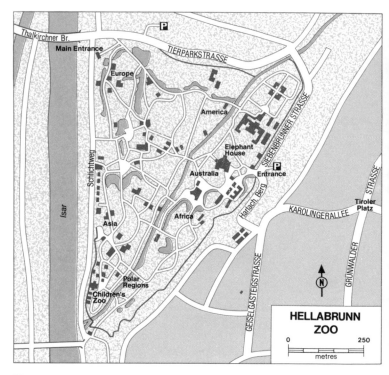

HELLABRUNN ZOO

0   250
metres

Excursions in the Surrounding Areas

A number of places of great cultural and historical interest can be easily reached from Munich by S-Bahn. These places are mentioned below. For more information about works of art and places of natural beauty in Upper Bavaria see Polyglott Travel Guides "Oberbayern/Westlicher Teil", "Oberbayern/Östlicher Teil", "Bayerische Alpen" and "Allgäu/Bayerisch-Schwaben", as well as the large Polyglott Travel Guide "Oberbayern".

ISARTAL (ISAR VALLEY)

Grünwald (25 tram, S-Bahn 10 to Höllriegelskreuth). As early as Celtic and Roman times fortifications were built above the banks of the Isar. In 1293 the Wittelsbachs built a *castle* here, where Emperor Ludwig the Bavarian (1287−1347) spent his youth and which was given its present form in the 15th century (castle museum).

Kloster Schäftlarn or Schäftlarn monastery (S-Bahn 10 to Hohenschäftlarn). This famous Benedictine abbey was founded already in 782. The present complex was erected in 1702−1757, the monastery buildings according to plans by Giovanni Antonio Viscardi, the *monastery church* at first according to drafts by François Cuvilliés, later on by those of Johann Baptist Gunezrhainer. The stucco work was by Johann Baptist Zimmermann. Johann Baptist Straub created the altars and the pulpit.

STARNBERGER SEE (LAKE OF STARNBERG)

The chief town of the 20-km-long and up to 5-km-wide lake (regular boat service in summer) is

Starnberg (618 m; pop. 17,500; S-Bahn 6), located north of the lake. The town grew up round a medieval castle. A boldly curved bridge leads from the *castle* (1541, now seat of a revenue office) to the *Old Parish Church of St. Joseph* (1770), a charming late rococo building. The high altar of this church is by Ignaz Günther.

Bernried has become known for its former *Augustinian canons' convent,* dating back to a double monastery founded in 1121. The *St. Martin's Church* has a carved wooden winged altar dating from 1484.

Berg has a *castle* built in 1640 and renovated several times, which now serves as residence for the hereditary Prince Albrecht von Bayern. The late Romanesque church contains the wooden relief "Death of the Virgin" from the 15th century. On the bank of the lake is the neo-Romanesque *Memorial Chapel* (1900) for Ludwig II, who found a tragic end here in the lake on June 13th 1886 at a place now marked by a cross.

AMMERSEE (AMMER LAKE)

Herrsching (56 m; pop. 8,400; S-Bahn 5) is the main town in the Ammersee region. The lake (regular boat service in summer) is 16 km long and up to 6 km wide. On the ridge of a moraine, above Herrsching, is the "Heiliger Berg" (or "Holy Mountain") with the

*Benediktinerabtei Andechs (Benedictine Abbey of Andechs). The **Kloster- und Wallfahrtskirche Mariä Verkündigung* (Monastery and Pilgrimage Church of the Annunciation) stands on a site formerly occupied by the castle belonging to the Counts of Andechs. The church was begun in 1438 and was given its baroque form in 1751.

The baroque *interior decorations* are by Johann Baptist Zimmermann. Very impressive is the **high altar* with the miraculous image of the Virgin enthroned. Andechs is also world famous for its monastic brewery.

On the southwest bank of the lake (bus and boat connections) lies

Dießen (538 m; pop. 7,500). It is dominated by the **Marienkirche* (St. Mary's Church), once belonging to the Augustinian Canons and erected by Johann Michael Fischer in 1732−1739. The *ceiling paintings* were created by Johann Georg Bergmüller. The stucco was the work of Johann Michael Feichtmayr. François Cuvilliés designed the ***high altar*, which was then completed by Joachim Dietrich. Worth noting are also the pulpit by Johann Baptist Straub and the angel figure by the famous sculptor Ignaz Günther.

FÜRSTENFELDBRUCK

About 23 km west of Munich on the Amper river is the town

Fürstenfeldbruck (528 m; pop. 31,000; S-Bahn 4). The *Kirche Mariä Himmelfahrt* (Church of Mary's Ascension) was begun in 1701 according to plans by Giovanni Antonio Viscardi and completed in 1718−1736 by Johann Georg Ettenhofer. The frescoes were the work of the two brothers Asam. The stucco was by Egid Quirin Asam, who also designed the high altar. The two statues of Ludwig the Stern and Ludwig the Bavarian were created by Roman Anton Boos.

DACHAU AND ENVIRONS

18 km northwest of Munich on the steep bank of the Amper river is the town of

Dachau (505 m; pop. 35,000; S-Bahn 2). In the 11th century a subsidiary line of the Wittelsbachs, Scheyern-Dachau, built a castle here, around which the place developed. In 1391 it became a market, in 1934 a town. The present *castle* is all that remains of a four-winged Renaissance building, erected by the Dukes Wilhelm IV and Albrecht V, according to plans by Heinrich Schöttl. The renovation work in 1715 was supervised by Dachau-born Joseph Effner. At the beginning of the 19th century the complex fell into ruin with the exception of the southwest tract. The *Parish Church of St. Jakob* was built in its present form in 1624−1625 according to a plan by Hans Krumper. On the eastern edge of the town there is a *place of remembrance* for one of the Third Reich's most barbarous concentration camps. The complex, laid out as a memorial in 1965, has a *museum* with about 500 objects documenting the horrors of the Dachau and other concentration camps.

Markt Indersdorf (460 m; pop. 6,600; S-Bahn 2). The foundation of the monastery formerly belonging to the Augustinian Canons dates back to a donation by Duke Otto VI of the Palatinate (about 1120). The late Romanesque *monastery church* was redone in baroque style in the middle of the 18th century. Worth seeing are the *high altar* decorated with figures by Andreas Faistenberger and a wall painting by Johann Andreas Wolff (1691).

Petersberg (connection with S-Bahn 2). The former *Benedictine Monastery Church of St. Peter,* built between 1104 and 1107, is one of the most beautiful Romanesque churches still existing in Bavaria. The frescoes of the choir deserve special attention.

Altomünster (connection with S-Bahn 2). As early as 750 the Benedictine double monastery of St. Alto was founded. Since 1485 it has served the Order of St. Birgit (it is the only St. Birgit convent in Germany). The construction of the *monastery church* was begun by Johann Michael Fischer in 1763. Worth seeing is the interior decoration, which was partly completed by Johann Baptist Staub und Jakob Rauch.

SCHLEISSHEIM

About 15 km north of Munich, easily accessible via the Nuremberg Autobahn or S-Bahn 1, is the suburb Schleißheim, worth visiting because of its palaces.

Altes Schloß or Old Palace. In its oldest form the palace dates back to Duke Wilhelm V, who had a hermitage built for himself here. Next to it he established a farm, which still today is used as a state and teaching domain. In 1616 Duke Maximilian I bought the manor Schleißheim from his father for a life annuity and commissioned various artists with the building of a palace. He was fortunate in being able to obtain the services of Heinrich Schön as an architect, who had already worked at the Munich Residence, and of Peter Candid as an artist for the interior furnishings. In 1623, when Duke Maximilian I was granted the electorate, the residence built in Italian style was completed. The Renaissance palace was almost totally destroyed in the Second World War. The present building dates from the years 1971−1972. It is not open to the public.

Parallel to the Old Palace, a little bit further to the east, Elector Maximilian II Emanuel had the

*Neues Schloß or New Palace built. As early as 1693 Enrico Zuccalli submitted the first plans, in which the New Palace was only to be the eastern end of a four-winged complex also including the Old Palace. The confusion of the War of the Spanish Succession (1704−1714) brought the construction to a standstill. It was not until 1719 that Joseph Effner was commissioned to continue building the New Palace. For the interior decorations he engaged among others François Cuvilliés the Elder, Johann Baptist Zimmermann and Charles Claude Debut, who were responsible for the stucco work. Cosmas Damian Asam, Franz Joachim Bleich and Nikolaus Gottfried Stuber worked on frescoes and paintings. Johann Adam Pichler was responsible for sculptural works. In 1763 Ignaz Günther decorated the wings of the east portal with fine allegorical adornments. The *staircase was completed by Leo von Klenze in the early 19th century. Klenze had redone the whole palace in a neo-classical style. However, none of these alterations are to be seen anymore, since the reconstruction after the Second World War was carried out according to the plans of Joseph Effner.

Apart from the artistically decorated rooms the *baroque gallery in the New Palace is of particular importance. The picture gallery is part of the Bavarian State Picture Collection. There was not enough room for all of it in the Old Pinakothek in Munich. Dutch and Flemish painters like Rubens, Brouwer, Ruisdael, van Goyen, Italian and French painters, as well as German ones like von Aachen, Schönfeld, and Lischka are represented here.

The Gobelin tapestries, entirely preserved, are of especial value too. They were acquired by Elector Maximilian II Emanuel, then governor of the Netherlands, from Flemish manufactures before 1700.

The eastern counterpart to the New Palace is the

*Gartenschloß Lustheim or Garden Palace Lustheim, built by Enrico Zuccalli in 1684—1688 as a wedding gift of Elector Maximilian II Emanuel to his wife Maria Antonia. For the interior frescoes artists like Johann Anton Gumpp, Francesco Rosa and Johann Andreas Trubillio could be engaged. Lustheim Palace today houses a *collection of Meißen porcelain, donated to the state in 1968 by Ernst Schneider, on the condition that it be only displayed in a baroque setting. The

*Park was laid out after 1693; for in this year Enrico Zuccalli, having been commissioned with the planning of the park, toured Holland to study garden architecture. Dominique Girard, who had earlier had a share in the lay-out of the Nymphenburg Park, was probably decisively

involved in the arrangement of this French park as well. The cascade of the canal, extending as far as Lustheim Palace, dates from 1724—1725.

Haimhausen (S-Bahn 1 to Lohhof, then 393 bus). The *palace, now housing an antique show, was built towards the end of the 17th century and was redone by François Cuvilliés the Elder in 1747.

FREISING AND ENVIRONS

33 km north of Munich, easily accessible via the road to Freimann or S-Bahn 1, is

Freising (471 m; pop. 30,000). Already in the 8th century the bishops St. Corbinian, St. Boniface and Arbeo worked here. The monastery had its golden age under Bishop Otto von Freising, uncle of Emperor Friedrich I Barbarossa (1152—1190). On the Domberg stands the originally Romanesque *Basilica St. Mary and St. Corbinian (about 1100). The church with nave and two aisles has undergone considerable alterations at various times. The crypt, which contains the shrine of St. Corbinian, has completely retained its Romanesque character. The Bestiensäule ("the beast pillar") is also worth seeing. In 1724 the brothers Asam redid the church with new stucco work and paintings.

The Monastery Church Neustift, north of Freising, was built by Giovanni Antonio Viscardi in 1705—1715. The decorations are by Johann Baptist Zimmermann and Franz Xaver Feichtmayr. Ignaz Günther constructed the high altar in 1765.

The former Benedictine Abbey Weihenstephan is now the seat of the agricultural and brewery faculties of Munich Technical University. The brewery, founded in 1146, is the world's oldest brewery still in existence. It has a pleasant beer garden.

Scheyern (Autobahn Nuremberg, 48 km north of Munich). About 1080 Haziga von Scheyern, wife of Count Otto, founded a Benedictine monastery here. The three-aisled late Romanesque *Klosterkirche Mariä Himmelfahrt (Monastery Church of Mary's Ascension) was altered greatly in the 16th and 18th centuries. In 1760 Ignaz Günther designed the statues on both sides of the high altar. Worth seeing is the Scheyern Cross, a Byzantine cross reliquary, for which Johann Georg Herkomer designed a glorious pyx in 1738.

Index

Accomodation 15
Almeida-Palais 43
Alte Akademie 23
Alte Pinakothek 12, 46
Alter Botanischer Garten 44
Altes Hackenviertel 28
Altes Rathaus 26
Altes Residenztheater (Cuvilliéstheater) 36
Altomünster 62
Amalienburg 56
Ammersee 61
Andechs, Monastery 61
Asam-Schlößchen 58
Auer Dult 5
Augustinerkirche, former 25

Badenburg 56
Bavaria (statue) 54
Bavaria-Film-Tours 13
Bayerisches Hauptmünzamt 31
Bayerisches Nationalmuseum 12, 52
Bayerische Staatsbibliothek (State Library) 41
Berg 61
Bernried 61
Blutenburg, Palace 57, 58
BMW-Museum 12, 59
Botanischer Garten 56
Breweries 13
Bürgersaal 23
Burgmuseum Grünwald 12

Cabarets 20
Camping 15
Concerts 20

Dachau 62
Deutsches Jagdmuseum 12, 25
Deutsches Museum 12, 32
Deutsches Theatermuseum 12
Die Neue Sammlung 12
Dießen 61
Dreifaltigkeitskirche 44

Englischer Garten 42
Erzbischöfliches Palais (Archbishop's Palace) 43
Evening entertainment 19

Feldherrnhalle 39
Food and drink 16
Frauenkirche 25
Freising 63
Friedensengel 53
Fürstenfeldbruck 62
Fürstenried, Palace 58

Glyptothek 12, 45
Grünwald 61
Gunezrhainerhaus 44

Haimhausen, Palace 63
Haus der Kunst 51
Heiliggeistkirche 29
Heilig Kreuz (Forstenried) 58
Hofbräuhaus 31
Hotels 15

Ignaz-Günther-Haus 29
Information 13
Isartal 61
Isartor 32

Karlsplatz (Stachus) 23
Karlstor 23
Karmeliterkirche 44
Königsplatz 45

Leuchtenberg-Palais 40
Lustheim, Palace 63

Magdalenenklause 56
Marienplatz 25
Mariensäule 26
Markt Indersdorf 62
Marstallmuseum 56
Maximilianeum 50
Maximilianstraße 49
Max-Joseph-Platz 34
Max-Monument 50

Messegelände (Fair grounds) 54
Michaelskirche 24
Münchner Stadtmuseum 12, 29

Nationaltheater 34
Neue Pinakothek 12, 47
Neues Rathaus 26
Nightclubs 20
Nymphenburg, Palace 55

Obelisk 45
Odeonsplatz 39
Oktoberfest 6, 54
Olympiapark 58
Olympiastadion 59

Pagodenburg 56
Palais Gise 44
Palais Montgelas 44
Palais Porcia 44
Palais Seinsheim 44
Prähistorische Staatssammlung (Prehistoric State Collection) 12, 53
Preysing-Palais (Residenzstraße) 39
Preysing-Palais (Prannerstraße) 44
Prinz-Carl-Palais 51
Prinzregentenstraße 50
Propyläen 46

Residenz 34
Residenzmuseum 12, 36
Restaurants 16
Ruhmeshalle 54

Salvatorkirche 43
St. Bonifaz 45
St. Georg (Bogenhausen) 57
St. Johann Nepomuk (Asamkirche) 28
St. Ludwig 41
St. Maria (Ramersdorf) 57
St. Michael (Berg am Laim) 57
St. Paul 54
St. Peter 27
St. Stephan (Berg am Laim) 57
St. Wolfgang (Pipping) 57

Schackgalerie, 12, 53
Schäftlarn, Monastery 61
Schatzkammer der Residenz (Treasury) 12, 36
Scheyern 63
Schleißheim, Palace 62
Schwabing 42
Sendlinger Tor 28
Siegestor 42
Siemens Museum 12
Sightseeing Tours 14
Sports 14
Staatliche Antikensammlungen 12, 46
Staatliche Graphische Sammlung 12, 45
Staatliche Sammlung Ägyptischer Kunst (Egyptian Art) 12
Staatsgalerie Moderner Kunst (Modern Art) 12, 51
Städtische Galerie im Lenbachhaus 12, 46
Starnberg 61
Starnberger See 61
Stuckvilla 53
Suresnes-Schlößchen 58

Television tower (Olympic tower) 58
Theatinerkirche 39
Theatres 19
Theresienwiese 54
Transport 21

University 42

Valentin-Musäum 12, 32
Viktualienmarkt 29
Völkerkundemuseum (Ethnological Museum) 12, 49

Weihenstephan 63
Westpark 54
Wittelsbacherplatz 43

Zoo 60